"YOU ARE THE LIGHT OF THE WORLD" (MATTHEW 5:14)

Statements on Mission by the World Council of Churches
1980-2005

"YOU ARE
THE LIGHT
OF THE WORLD"

*Statements on Mission by the
World Council of Churches
1980-2005*

WCC Publications, Geneva

Fevru AF 4/09 15.00

Cover design: Marie Arnaud Snakkers

ISBN 2-8254-1435-2

© 2005 World Council of Churches
P.O. Box 2100, 150 route de Ferney
1211 Geneva 2, Switzerland
Web site: http://www.wcc-coe.org

Printed in France

Table of Contents

Introduction

"Evangelism is the test of true ecumenism," according to Philip Potter, general secretary of the World Council of Churches (WCC) from 1972 to 1984.[1]

The basis of the WCC clearly relates ecumenism, mission and common witness:

> The World Council of Churches is a fellowship of churches which confess the Lord Jesus Christ as God and Saviour according to the scriptures and therefore seek to fulfil together their common calling to the glory of the one God, Father, Son and Holy Spirit.[2]

These are clear affirmations, but what does mission or evangelism mean in ecumenical theology and practice?

One way to discover it is to follow the journey of the world mission conferences which the WCC organizes every seven or eight years. In fact, one of the major roots of the contemporary ecumenical movement is to be found in the world mission conference held in 1910 in Edinburgh, Scotland, which gave birth, some years later, to the International Missionary Council. The IMC merged with the WCC in 1961, and since then ecumenical mission work has been carried out under the auspices of the Commission and Conference on World Mission and Evangelism (CWME) and its related staff team.[3]

Another way to discover what mission and evangelism mean in ecumenical theology and practice is to study, compare and comment the declarations or statements on mission and evangelism published at irregular intervals by the WCC. This book serves as a resource for this second approach and presents all the recent mission statements produced since 1980 by the WCC:

- Mission and Evangelism: An Ecumenical Affirmation (1982)
- Towards Common Witness: A Call to Adopt Responsible Relationships in Mission and to Renounce Proselytism (1997)
- Mission and Evangelism in Unity Today (2000)
- Mission as Ministry of Reconciliation (2005)
- The Healing Mission of the Church (2005)

These statements do not all have the same authority, and separate presentations clearly indicate what their status is in terms of their adoption by a governing or advisory body. However, read together they provide a fair picture of the main theses and emphases of ecumenical missiology. It is our opinion that they have not received the considered they deserve both within and without the ecumenical movement, with exception perhaps of the 1982 declaration which was widely appreciated.

We have chosen the text of Matthew 5:14, "You are the light of the world", as the title of this book for several reasons. For the first time in the gospels, the Lord qualifies all his disciples as a community whose essence and mandate is not for itself, but for the world. This is the first mission proclamation and commission. Together with the parallel sentence "you are the salt of the earth", it provides a key turning point in the Sermon on the Mount, linking the proclamation of the good news as beatitudes with the guidelines that follow for a gospel-based ethics and spirituality. This sentence and title summarizes the ecumenical approach to mission reflected in the WCC statements collected in this book. It is a vision which combines the search for the justice God requires and a shining witness to Christ, a mission whose aim is to invite all people to give glory to God (Matt. 5:16).

Published just prior to the world mission conference in Athens, May 2005, this book will contribute to providing a solid missiological basis for reflection and sharing on the conference theme. This theme combines a confession and vision of God's overall mission, understood in terms of healing and reconciliation, with the call to the churches to participate by forming, renewing and multiplying communities shaped by and sharing the gospel.

Come, Holy Spirit, heal and reconcile!
Called in Christ to be reconciling and healing communities

Jacques Matthey
Programme Executive for Mission Studies
World Council of Churches

---

[1] Address on "Mission, Evangelism and the World Council of Churches", US Conference of Churches, 1970, quoted by Michael N. Jagessar, *Full of Life for All, The Work and Theology of Philip A. Potter. A Historical Survey and Systematic Analysis of Major Themes*, Zoetermeer, Uitgeverij Bvoekencentrum, 1997, p.207.

[2] Constitution article 1, italics added.

[3] Introductions to the world mission conferences can be found in the *Dictionary of the Ecumenical Movement*, 2nd ed., Nicholas Lossky et al. eds, WCC, 2002, and in *A History of the Ecumenical Movement*, three volumes (1517-1948; 1948-1968; 1968-2000), WCC. One can also follow the developments by consulting the volumes of the *International Review of Mission*, published quarterly since 1912.

Mission and Evangelism: An Ecumenical Affirmation

Presentation

The Ecumenical Affirmation (EA) is and remains the official WCC position on mission and evangelism. It was approved by the central committee in 1982 and commended to the churches for their study and implementation. As is usual with ecumenical documents, it has no authority except the intrinsic truth of its content and is not binding for any church, whether or not a member of the WCC. It is the ecumenical contribution and response to the missiological debate of the time, expressed in several important documents, such as the Lausanne Covenant (1974) and the encyclical Evangelii Nuntiandi (1975).[1]

The EA can be interpreted as a follow-up of the debate on mission and evangelism held at the WCC assembly in Nairobi in 1975.[2] A WCC statement on mission had been requested by the central committee in 1976. After an unsuccessful attempt at producing such a text at the world mission conference in Melbourne 1980,[3] the then director of the Commission on World Mission and Evangelism, Emilio Castro, wrote a first draft, which after many discussions and revisions came to be debated at the central committee in 1981, before the revised final version could be approved one year later.

The EA is rightly considered a successful result of ecumenical conversations, involving missiologists and mission practitioners from various church and spiritual affiliations, including Roman Catholic, Orthodox and evangelical. In his testimony to the central committee, Bishop Anastasios Yannoulatos, missiology professor in Greece at that time, acknowledged that ecumenical achievement by saying, "I find that the paper is the result of a real theological and spiritual interconfessional fermentation of a very constructive type."[4] Elaborated in cooperation with persons coming from a great variety of mission involvements, it was well received in many places.

More than many other documents of the WCC, the EA has a holistic, encompassing approach to mission, highlighting both the call to a clear witness to Jesus Christ and the promised kingdom of God, as well as the mandate to live in solidarity with those exploited and rejected by social and economic systems. It has become famous also for its double credibility criterion for Christian witness:

> There is no evangelism without solidarity; there is no Christian solidarity that does not involve sharing the knowledge of the kingdom which is God's promise to the poor of the earth. There is here a double credibility test: a proclamation that does not hold forth the promises of the justice of the kingdom to the poor of the earth is a caricature of the gospel; but Christian participation in the struggles for justice which does not point towards the promises of the kingdom also makes a caricature of a Christian understanding of justice.[5]

This is formulated in the terms of the 1980s, still very much influenced by the debates of the world mission conference in Melbourne, Australia, in 1980. In its essence, the test remains valid for Christian mission in any time and place, even if the formulation itself could be revised to respond to various contextual challenges. At the worldwide level, however, it still makes sense today.

The EA is built on a trinitarian basis with a Christological concentration and presents mission not just as an activity of the church, but the church itself as a function of the mission of God in the world. It carries strong paragraphs on personal and community conversion, together with the recognition of the missionary importance of worship and the eucharist. While it is clear on the social involvement which must be part of the church's mission, the document also affirms the importance of planting local congregations as essential to Christian mission strategy, "until there is, in every human community, a cell of the kingdom, a church confessing Jesus Christ and in his name serving the gospel".[6] It also acknowledges the role of those witnesses who cross cultural frontiers, and calls for an understanding of them not as an alibi to prevent the local mission of the church, but as a symbolic concentration of the missionary vocation of the whole church.[7] Local and worldwide mission are linked and must not be in opposition to each other.

Finally, the EA also coins the expression "mission in Christ's way" which remains an essential criterion for discernment: no missionary method is neutral. It "illustrates or betrays the gospel".[8] This call remains of utmost relevance in the new millennium and challenges every Christian witness, including the way ecumenical organizations or churches do or do not act in matters of evangelism, mission, pastoral care, liturgy, prophecy or development.

More than twenty years after its approval, the EA remains a milestone on the WCC's journey towards true common witness and proves, as one of the central committee members of 1982 said, how the integration of the IMC and the WCC resulted in a true maturity of relationship between "mission" and "church".

JM

[1] The Lausanne Covenant, International Congress on World Evangelization, Lausanne 1974. Many publications, cf. e.g. Michael Kinnamon et al. eds, *The Ecumenical Movement: An Anthology of Key Texts and Voices*, WCC Publications, and Grand Rapids MI, Eerdmans, 1997, pp.358-63. *Evangelii Nuntiandi*, various publications, also on Internet: http://www.vatican.va/holy_father/paul_vi/apost_exhortations/index.htm

[2] David M. Paton ed., *Breaking Barriers:* Nairobi 1975, London, SPCK and Grand Rapids MI, Eerdmans, 1976, in particular the reference to the address by Mortimer Arias and the response by John Stott, pp.17-19.

[3] However, the deliberations and results of the Melbourne conference influenced many formulations and theses of the Ecumenical Affirmation, both on the matter of Christian witness and solidarity, as well as on evangelism and ecclesiology.

[4] In his testimony presented to the 1982 session of the central committee, published in: *IRM,* vol. 71, no. 284, Oct. 1982, p.452. The whole issue of IRM is dedicated to the Ecumenical Affirmation.

[5] EA, §34.

[6] EA, §25.

[7] EA, §39.

[8] EA, §28.

Mission and Evangelism: An Ecumenical Affirmation

Preface

The biblical promise of a new earth and a new heaven where love, peace and justice will prevail (Ps. 85:7-13; Isa. 32:17-18, 65:17-25 and Rev. 21:1-2) invites our actions as Christians in history. The contrast of that vision with the reality of today reveals the monstrosity of human sin, the evil unleashed by the rejection of God's liberating will for humankind. Sin, alienating persons from God, neighbour and nature, is found both in individual and corporate forms, both in slavery of the human will and in social, political and economic structures of domination and dependence.

The church is sent into the world to call people and nations to repentance, to announce forgiveness of sin and a new beginning in relations with God and with neighbours through Jesus Christ. This evangelistic calling has a new urgency today.

In a world where the number of people who have no opportunity to know the story of Jesus is growing steadily, *how necessary it is to multiply the witnessing vocation of the church!*

In a world where the majority of those who do not know Jesus are the poor of the earth, those to whom he promised the kingdom of God, *how essential it is to share with them the Good News of that kingdom!*

In a world where people are struggling for justice, freedom and liberation, often without the realization of their hopes, *how important it is to announce that God's kingdom is promised to them!*

In a world where the marginalized and the drop-outs of affluent society search desperately for comfort and identity in drugs or esoteric cults, *how imperative it is to announce that he has come so that all may have life and may have it in all its fullness* (John 10:10)!

In a world where so many find little meaning, except in the relative security of their affluence, *how necessary it is to hear once again Jesus' invitation to discipleship, service and risk!*

In a world where so many Christians are nominal in their commitment to Jesus Christ, *how necessary it is to call them again to the fervour of their first love!*

In a world where wars and rumours of war jeopardize the present and future of humankind, where an enormous part of natural resources and people are consumed in the arms race, *how crucial it is to call the peace-makers blessed, convinced that God in Christ has broken all barriers and has reconciled the world to himself* (Eph. 2:14; 2 Cor. 5:19)!

This ecumenical affirmation is a challenge which the churches extend to each other to announce that God reigns, and that there is hope for a future when God will "unite all things in him, things in heaven and things on earth" (Eph. 1:10). Jesus is "the first and last, and the Living One" (Rev. 1:17-18), who "is coming soon" (Rev. 22:12), who "makes all things new" (Rev. 21:5).

The Call to Mission

1. The present ecumenical movement came into being out of the conviction of the churches that the division of Christians is a scandal and an impediment to the witness of the church. **There is a growing awareness among the churches today of the inextricable relationship between Christian unity and missionary calling, between ecumenism and evangelization. "Evangelization is the test of our ecumenical vocation."**[1]

As "a fellowship of churches which confess the Lord Jesus Christ as God and Saviour, according to the scriptures, and therefore seek to fulfil together their common calling to the glory of the one God, Father, Son and Holy Spirit",[2] the rallying point of the World Council of Churches is the common confession of Jesus Christ. The saving ministry of the Son is understood within the action of the Holy Trinity; it was the Father who in the power of the Spirit sent Jesus Christ the Son of God incarnate, the Saviour of the whole world. The churches of the WCC are on a pilgrimage towards unity under the missionary vision of John 17:21, "that they may all be one; even as thou, Father, art in me, and I in thee, that they also may be in us, so that the world may believe that thou hast sent me".[3]

2. Already in the Old Testament the people of Israel were looking forward to the day of peace where God's justice will prevail (Isa. 11:1-9). Jesus came into that tradition announcing that the kingdom of God was at hand (Mark 1:15), that in him the reality of the kingdom was present (Luke 4:15-21). God was offering this new justice to the children, to the poor, to all who labour and are heavy laden, to all those who will repent and will follow Jesus. The early church confessed Jesus as Lord, as the highest authority at whose name every knee shall bow, who in the cross and in the resurrection has liberated in this world the power of sacrificial love.

3. Christ sent the disciples with the words: "As the Father has sent me, even so I send you" (John 20:21). The disciples of Jesus were personal witnesses of the risen Christ (1 John 1:2-3). As such, they were sent - commissioned apostles to the world. **Based on their testimony which is preserved in the New Testament and in the life of the church, the church has as one constitutive mark its being apostolic, its being sent into the world** (appendix 1). God in Christ has equipped the church with all gifts of the Spirit necessary for its witness. "You shall receive power when the Holy Spirit has come upon you; and you shall be my witnesses in Jerusalem, and in all Judaea and Samaria, and to the end of the earth" (Acts 1:8).

4. The book of Acts tells the story of the expansion of the early church as it fulfils its missionary vocation. The Holy Spirit came upon that small Jerusalem community on the day of Pentecost (Acts 2:1-39), in order that through them and through others

who were to believe in Christ through their word (John 17:20), the world may be healed and redeemed.

The early church witnessed to its Risen Lord in a variety of ways, most specially in the style of life of its members. "And day by day, attending the temple together and breaking bread in their homes, they partook of food with glad and generous hearts, praising God and having favour with all the people. And the Lord added to their number day by day those who were being saved" (Acts 2:46-47) (appendix 2). **Through the persecutions suffered by the early Christians, the word spread spontaneously**: "Now those who were scattered went about preaching the word" (Acts 8:4). The apostles then came to confirm the faith of those who had accepted the word of God (Acts 8:14-17). **At other times, the word spread through more explicit and purposeful ministries.** The church in Antioch organized the first missionary trip. Barnabas and Paul were sent by the church in response to the Holy Spirit (Acts 13:1-4). Time and time again, the church was surprised by God's calling to face entirely new missionary situations (Acts 8:26, 10:17, 16:9-10).

5. Jesus Christ was in himself the complete revelation of God's love, manifested in justice and forgiveness through all aspects of his earthly life. He completed the work of the Father. "My food is to do the will of him who sent me, and to accomplish his work" (John 4:34). In his obedience to the Father's will, in his love for humanity, he used many ways to reveal God's love to the world: forgiving, healing, casting out demons, teaching, proclaiming, denouncing, testifying in courts, finally surrendering his life. The church today has the same freedom to develop its mission, to respond to changing situations and circumstances (appendix 3). It is sent into the world, participating in that flow of love from God the Father. In that mission of love (Matt. 22:37) through all aspects of ifs life, the church endeavours to witness to the full realization of God's kingdom in Jesus Christ. The church is called, like John the Baptist, to point towards the "lamb of God who takes away the sin of the world" (John 1:29).

The Call to Proclamation and Witness

6. The mission of the church ensues from the nature of the church as the body of Christ, sharing in the ministry of Christ as Mediator between God and his creation. This mission of mediation in Christ involves two integrally related movements - one from God to creation, and the other from creation to God. The church manifests God's love for the world in Christ - through word and deed, in identification with all humanity, in loving service and joyful proclamation; the church, in that same identification with all humanity, lifts up to God its pain and suffering, hope and aspiration, joy and thanksgiving in intercessory prayer and eucharistic worship. Any imbalance between these two directions of the mediatory movement adversely affects our ministry and mission in the world.

Only a church fully aware of how people in the world live and feel and think can adequately fulfil either aspect of this mediatory mission. It is at this point that the church recognizes the validity and significance of the ministry of others to the church, in order that the church may better understand and be in closer solidarity with the world, knowing and sharing its pains and yearnings. Only by responding attentively to others can we remove our ignorance and misunderstanding of others, and be better able to minister to them.

At the very heart of the church's vocation in the world is the proclamation of the kingdom of God inaugurated in Jesus the Lord, crucified and risen. Through its internal life of eucharistic worship, thanksgiving, intercessory prayer, through planning for mission and evangelism, through a daily life-style of solidarity with the poor, through advocacy even to confrontation with the powers that oppress human beings, the churches are trying to fulfil this evangelistic vocation.

7. **The starting point of our proclamation is Christ and Christ crucified**. "We preach Christ crucified, a stumbling

block to Jews and folly to Gentiles" (1 Cor. 1:23). The good news handed on to the Church is that God's grace was in Jesus Christ, who "though he was rich, yet for your sake he became poor, so that by his poverty you might become rich" (2 Cor. 8:9).

Following human wisdom, the wise men from the Orient who were looking for the child went to the palace of King Herod. They did not know that "there was no place for him in the inn" and that he was born in a manger, poor among the poor. He even went so far in his identification with the poverty of humankind that his family was obliged to take the route of political refugee to Egypt. He was raised as a worker, came proclaiming God's caring for the poor, announced blessedness for them, sided with the underprivileged, confronted the powerful and went to the cross to open up a new life for humankind. As his disciples, we announce his solidarity with all the downtrodden and marginalized. Those who are considered to be nothing are precious in God's eyes (1 Cor. 1:26-31). **To believe in Jesus the King is to accept his undeserved grace and enter with him into the kingdom, taking sides with the poor struggling to overcome poverty. Both those who announce Jesus as the servant king and those who accept this announcement and respond to it are invited to enter with him daily in identification and participation with the poor of the earth.**

With the apostle Paul and all Christian churches, we confess Christ Jesus, "who, though he was in the form of God, did not court equality with God a thing to be grasped, but emptied himself, taking the form of a servant, being born in the likeness of men. And being found in human form he humbled himself and became obedient unto death, even death on a cross. Therefore God has highly exalted him and bestowed on him the name which is above every name, that at the name of Jesus every knee should bow, in heaven and on earth and under the earth, and every tongue confess that Jesus Christ is Lord, to the glory of God the Father" (Phil. 2:6-11).

8. But Christ's identification with humanity went even more deeply, and while nailed on the cross accused as a political criminal, he took upon himself the guilt even of those who crucified him. "Father, forgive them; for they know not what they do" (Luke 23:34). The Christian confession reads, "For our sake he made him to be sin who knew no sin, so that in him we might become the righteousness of God" (2 Cor. 5:21). The cross is the place of the decisive battle between the powers of evil and the love of God. It uncovers the lostness of the world, the magnitude of human sinfulness, the tragedy of human alienation. The total self-surrendering of Christ reveals the immeasurable depth of God's love for the world (John 3:16).

On this same cross, Jesus was glorified. Here God the Father glorified the Son of man, and in so doing confirmed Jesus as the Son of God (John 13:31). "The early Christians used many analogies to describe what they had experienced and what they believed had happened. The most striking picture is that of a sacrificed lamb, slaughtered but yet living, sharing the throne, which symbolized the heart of all power and sovereignty, with the living God himself." [4]

It is this Jesus that the church proclaims as the very life of the world because on the cross he gave his own life for all that all may live. In him misery, sin and death are defeated once forever. They cannot be accepted as having final power over human life. In him there is abundant life, life eternal. **The church proclaims Jesus, risen from the dead. Through the resurrection, God vindicates Jesus, and opens up a new period of missionary obedience until he comes again** (Acts 1:11). The power of the risen and crucified Christ is now released. It is the new birth to a new life, because as he took our predicament on the cross, he also took us into a new life in his resurrection. "When anyone is united to Christ, there is a new creation; the old has passed away, behold, the new has come" (2 Cor. 5:17) (appendix 4).

Evangelism calls people to look towards that Jesus and commit their life to him, to enter into the kingdom whose king has come in the powerless child of Bethlehem, in the murdered one on the cross.

Ecumenical Convictions

9. In the ecumenical discussions and experience, churches with their diverse confessions and traditions and in their various expressions as parishes, monastic communities, religious orders, etc., have learned to recognize each other as participants in the one worldwide missionary movement. *Thus, together, they can affirm an ecumenical perception of Christian mission expressed in the following convictions under which they covenant to work for the kingdom or God.*

1. Conversion

10. The proclamation of the gospel includes an invitation to recognize and accept in a personal decision the saving lordship of Christ. It is the announcement of a personal encounter, mediated by the Holy Spirit, with the living Christ, receiving his forgiveness and making a personal acceptance of the call to discipleship and a life of service. God addresses himself specifically to each of his children, as well as to the whole human race. **Each person is entitled to hear the good news**. Many social forces today press for conformity and passivity. Masses of poor people have been deprived of their right to decide about their lives and the life of their society. While anonymity and marginalization seem to reduce the possibilities for personal decisions to a minimum, God as Father knows each one of his children and calls each of them to make a fundamental personal act of allegiance to him and his kingdom in the fellowship of his people.

11. While the basic experience of conversion is the same, the awareness of an encounter with God revealed in Christ, the concrete occasion of this experience and the actual shape of the same differs in terms of our personal situation. **The calling is to specific changes, to renounce evidences of the domination of**

sin in our lives and to accept responsibilities in terms of God's love for our neighbour. John the Baptist said very specifically to the soldiers what they should do; Jesus did not hesitate to indicate to the young ruler that his wealth was the obstacle to his discipleship.

> Conversion happens in the midst of our historical reality and incorporates the totality of our life, because God's love is concerned with that totality. Jesus' call is an invitation to follow him joyfully, to participate in his servant body, to share with him in the struggle to overcome sin, poverty and death.

12. The importance of this decision is highlighted by the fact that God himself through his Holy Spirit helps the acceptance of his offering of fellowship. The New Testament calls this a new birth (John 3:3). It is also called conversion, metanoia, total transformation of our attitudes and styles of life. Conversion as a dynamic and ongoing process "involves a turning *from* and a turning *to*. It always demands reconciliation, a new relationship both with God and with others. It involves leaving our old security behind (Matt. 16:24) and putting ourselves at risk in a life of faith."[5] It is "conversion *from* a life characterized by sin, separation from God, submission to evil and the unfulfilled potential of God's image, *to* a new life characterized by the forgiveness of sins, obedience to the commands of God, renewed fellowship with God in Trinity, growth in the restoration of the divine image and the realization... of the love of Christ..."[6]

The call to conversion, as a call to repentance and obedience, should also be addressed to nations, groups and families. To proclaim the need to change from war to peace, from injustice to justice, from racism to solidarity, from hate to love is a witness rendered to Jesus Christ and to his kingdom. The prophets of the Old Testament addressed themselves constantly to the collective conscience of the people of Israel calling the rulers and the people to repentance and to renewal of the covenant.

13. Many of those who are attracted to Christ are put off by what they see in the life of the churches as well as in individual Christians. How many of the millions of people in the world who are not confessing Jesus Christ have rejected him because of what they saw in the lives of Christians! **Thus the call to conversion should begin with the repentance of those who do the calling, who issue the invitation.** Baptism in itself is a unique act, the covenant that Christians no longer belong to themselves but have been bought forever with the blood of Christ and belong to God. But the experience of baptism should be constantly re-enacted by daily dying with Christ to sin, to themselves and to the world and rising again with him into the servant body of Christ to become a blessing for the surrounding community.

> The experience of conversion gives meaning to people in all stages of life, endurance to resist oppression, and assurance that even death has no final power over human life because God in Christ has already taken our life with him, a life that is "hidden with Christ in God" (Col. 3:3).

2. The gospel to all realms of life

14. In the Bible, religious Life was never limited to the temple or isolated from daily life (Hos. 6:4-6; Isa. 58:6-7). **The teaching of Jesus on the kingdom of God is a clear reference to God's loving lordship over all human history. We cannot limit our witness to a supposedly private area of life. The lordship of Christ is to be proclaimed to all realms of life.** In the Great Commission, Jesus said to his disciples, "All authority in heaven and on earth has been given to me. Go, therefore, and make disciples of all nations, baptizing them in the name of the Father and of the Son and of the Holy Spirit, teaching them to obey all that I have commanded you. And lo, I am with you always, to the close of the age" (Matt. 28:19-20). The good news of the kingdom is a challenge to the structures of society (Eph. 3:9-10, 6:12)

as well as a call to individuals to repent. "If salvation from sin through divine forgiveness is to be truly and fully personal, it must express itself in the renewal of these relations and structures. Such renewal is not merely a consequence but an essential element of the conversion of whole human beings."[7]

15. "The evangelistic witness is directed towards all of the ktisis (creation) which groans and travails in search of adoption and redemption... The transfiguring power of the Holy Trinity is meant to reach into every nook and cranny of our national life... The evangelistic witness will also speak to the structures of this world; its economic, political and societal institutions... We must re-learn the patristic lesson that the church is the mouth and voice of the poor and the oppressed in the presence of the powers that be. In our own way we must learn once again 'how to speak to the ear of the King', on the people's behalf... Christ was sent for no lesser purpose than bringing the world into the life of God."[8]

16. In the fulfilment of its vocation, the church is called to announce good news in Jesus Christ, forgiveness, hope, a new heaven and a new earth; *to denounce* powers and principalities, sin and injustice; *to console* the widows and orphans, healing, restoring the broken-hearted; and *to celebrate* life in the midst of death. In carrying out these tasks, churches may meet limitations, constraints, even persecution from prevailing powers which pretend to have final authority over the life and destiny of people.

17. In some countries there is pressure to limit religion to the private life of the believer - to assert that freedom to believe should be enough. The Christian faith challenges that assumption. **The church claims the right and the duty to exist publicly - visibly - and to address itself openly to issues of human concern.** "Confessing Christ *today* means that the Spirit makes us struggle with... sin and forgiveness, power and powerlessness, exploitation and misery, the universal search for identity,

the widespread loss of Christian motivation, and the spiritual longings of those who have not heard Christ's name. It means that we are in communion with the prophets who announced God's will and promise for humankind and society, with the martyrs who sealed their confession with suffering and death, and also with the doubtful who can only whisper their confession of the Name."[9]

18. The realm of science and technology deserves particular attention today. The everyday life of most children, women and men, whether rich or poor, is affected by the avalanche of scientific discoveries. Pharmaceutical science has revolutionized sexual behaviour. Increasingly sophisticated computers solve problems in seconds for which formerly a whole life-time was needed; at the same time they become a means of invading the privacy of millions of people. Nuclear power threatens the survival of life on this planet, while at the same time it provides a new source of energy. Biological research stands at the awesome frontier of interference with the genetic code which could - for better or for worse - change the whole human species. Scientists are, therefore, seeking ethical guidance. Behind the questions as to right or wrong decisions and attitudes, however, there are ultimate theological questions: What is the meaning of human existence? the goal of history? the true reality within and beyond what can be tested and quantified empirically? The ethical questions arise out of a quest for a new world-view, a faith.

19. The biblical stories and ancient creeds do furnish precious insights for witnessing to the gospel in the scientific world. Can theologians, however, with these insights, help scientists achieve responsible action in genetic engineering or nuclear physics? It would hardly seem possible so long as the great communication gap between these two groups persists. Those directly involved in and affected by scientific research can best discern and explicate the insights of Christian faith in terms of specific ethical positions.

Christian witness will point towards Jesus Christ in whom real humanity is revealed and who is in God's wisdom the centre of all creation, the "head over all things" (Eph. 1:10,22f.). This witness will show the glory and the humility of human stewardship on this earth.

3. The church and its unity in God's mission

20. To receive the message of the kingdom of God is to be incorporated into the body of Christ, the church, the author and sustainer of which is the Holy Spirit (appendix 5). The churches are to be a sign for the world. They are to intercede as he did, to serve as he did. **Thus Christian mission is the action of the body of Christ in the history of humankind - a continuation of Pentecost. Those who through conversion and baptism accept the gospel of Jesus partake in the life of the body of Christ and participate in an historical tradition.** Sadly there are many betrayals of this high calling in the history of the churches. Many who are attracted to the vision of the kingdom find it difficult to be attracted to the concrete reality of the church. They are invited to join in a continual process of renewal of the churches. "The challenge facing the churches is not that the modern world is unconcerned about their evangelistic message, but rather whether they are so renewed in their life and thought that they become a living witness to the integrity of the gospel. The evangelizing churches need themselves to receive the good news and to let the Holy Spirit remake their life when and how he wills"[10] (appendix 6).

21. The celebration of the eucharist is the place for the renewal of the missionary conviction at the heart of every congregation. According to the apostle Paul, the celebration of the eucharist is in itself a "proclamation of the death of the Lord until he comes" (1 Cor. 11:26). "In such ways God feeds his people as they celebrate the mystery of the eucharist so that they may confess in word and deed that Jesus Christ is Lord, to the glory of God the Father"[11] (appendix 7).

> The eucharist is bread for a missionary people. We acknowl-
> edge with deep sorrow the fact that Christians do not join
> together at the Lord's table. This contradicts God's will and
> impoverishes the body of Christ. The credibility of our
> Christian witness is at stake.

22. Christians are called to work for the renewal and transformation of the churches. Today there are many signs of the work of
the Holy Spirit in such a renewal. *The house gatherings of the
church in China or the basic ecclesial communities in Latin
America, the liturgical renewal, biblical renewal, the revival of
the monastic vocation, the charismatic movement, are indications of the renewal possibilities of the church of Jesus Christ.*

23. In the announcement to the world of the reconciliation in
Jesus Christ, churches are called to unity. Faced with the challenge and threat of the world, the churches often unite to defend
common positions. **But common witness should be the natural consequence of their unity with Christ in his mission.** The
ecumenical experience has discovered the reality of a deep spiritual unity. The common recognition of the authority of the
Bible and of the creeds of the ancient church and a growing convergence in doctrinal affirmations should allow the churches not
only to affirm together the fundamentals of the Christian faith,
but also to proclaim together the good news of Jesus Christ to
the world. In solidarity, churches are helping each other in their
respective witness before the world. In the same solidarity, they
should share their spiritual and material resources to announce
together and clearly their common hope and common calling.

24. "Often it is socially and politically more difficult to witness
together since the powers of this world promote division. In
such situations common witness is particularly precious and
Christ-like. Witness that dares to be common is a powerful sign
of unity coming directly and visibly from Christ and a glimpse
of his kingdom."[12]

The impulse for common witness comes from the depth of our faith. "Its urgency is underlined when we realize the seriousness of the human predicament and the tremendous task waiting for the churches at present".[13]

25. It is at the heart of Christian mission to foster the multiplication of local congregations in every human community. The planting of the seed of the gospel will bring forward a people gathered around the word and sacraments and called to announce God's revealed purpose.

Thanks to the faithful witness of disciples through the ages, churches have sprung up in practically every country. **This task of sowing the seed needs to be continued until there is, in every human community, a cell of the kingdom, a church confessing Jesus Christ and in his name serving his people.** The building up of the church in every place is essential to the gospel. The vicarious work of Christ demands the presence of a vicarious people. A vital instrument for the fulfilment of the missionary vocation of the church is the local congregation.

26. The planting of the church in different cultures demands a positive attitude towards inculturation of the gospel. Ancient churches, through centuries of intimate relations with the cultures and aspirations of their people, have proved the powerful witnessing character of this rooting of the churches in the national soil. "Inculturation has its source and inspiration in the mystery of the incarnation. The Word was made flesh. Here flesh means the fully concrete, human and created reality that Jesus was. Inculturation, therefore, becomes another way of describing Christian mission. If proclamation sees mission in the perspective of the Word to be proclaimed, inculturation sees mission in the perspective of the flesh, or concrete embodiment, which the Word assumes in a particular individual, community, institution or culture."[14]

Inculturation should not be understood merely as intellectual research; it occurs when Christians express their faith in the symbols and images of their respective culture. *The best way to stimulate the process of inculturation is to participate in the struggle of the less privileged for their liberation. Solidarity is the best teacher of common cultural values.*

27. This growing cultural diversity could create some difficulties. In our attempt to express the catholicity of the church we may lose the sense of its unity. **But the unity we look for is not uniformity but the multiple expression of a common faith and a common mission.**

"We have found this confession of Christ out of our various cultural contexts to be not only a mutually inspiring, but also a mutually corrective exchange. Without this sharing our individual affirmations would gradually become poorer and narrower. We need each other to regain the lost dimensions of confessing Christ and to discover dimensions unknown to us before. Sharing in this way, we are all changed and our cultures are transformed."[15]

The vision of nations coming from the East, the West, the North and the South to sit at the final banquet of the kingdom should always be before us in our missionary endeavour.

4. Mission in Christ's way

---

28. "As the Father has sent me, even so I send you" (John 20:21). The self-emptying of the servant who lived among the people, sharing in their hopes and sufferings, giving his life on the cross for all humanity - this was Christ's way of proclaiming the good news, and as disciples we are summoned to follow the same way. "A servant is not greater than his master; nor is he who is sent greater than he who sent him" (John 13:16).

Our obedience in mission should be patterned on the ministry and teaching of Jesus. He gave his love and his time to all people. He praised the widow who gave her last coin to the temple; he received Nicodemus during the night; he called Matthew to the apostolate; he visited Zacchaeus in his home; he gave himself in a special way to the poor, consoling, affirming and challenging them. He spent long hours in prayer and lived in dependence on and willing obedience to God's will.

An imperialistic crusader's spirit was foreign to him. **Churches are free to choose the ways they consider best to announce the gospel to different people in different circumstances. But these options are never neutral. Every methodology illustrates or betrays the gospel we announce. In all communications of the gospel, power must be subordinate to love.**

29. Our societies are undergoing a significant and rapid change under the impact of new communication technologies and their applications. We are entering the age of the information society, characterized by an ever increasing media presence in all relationships, both interpersonal and intersocial. Christians need to re-think critically their responsibility for all communication processes and re-define the values of Christian communications. In the use of all new media options, the communicating church must ensure that these instruments of communication are not masters, but servants in the proclaiming of the kingdom of God and its values. As servants, the new media options, kept within their own limits, will help to liberate societies from communication bondage and will place tools in the hands of communities for witnessing to Jesus Christ.

30. Evangelism happens in terms of interpersonal relations when the Holy Spirit quickens to faith. Through sharing the pains and joys of life, identifying with people, the gospel is understood and communicated.

Often, the primary confessors are precisely the non-publicized, unsensational people who gather together steadfastly in small caring communities, whose life prompts the question: "What is the source of the meaning of your life? What is the power of your

powerlessness?", giving the occasion to name THE NAME.
Shared experiences reveal how often Christ is confessed in the
very silence of a prison cell or of a restricted but serving, waiting, praying church.

Mission calls for a serving church in every land, a church which
is willing to be marked with the stigmata (nailmarks) of the crucified and risen Lord. In this way the church will show that it
belongs to that movement of God's love shown in Christ who
went to the periphery of life. Dying outside the gates of the city
(Heb. 13:12) he is the high priest offering himself for the salvation of the world. Outside the city gates the message of a self-
giving, sharing love is truly proclaimed, here the church renews
its vocation to be the body of Christ in joyful fellowship with its
risen Lord (1 John 3:16).

5. Good news to the poor

31. There is a new awareness of the growing gap between
wealth and poverty among the nations and inside each nation. It
is a cruel reality that the number of people who do not reach the
material level for a normal human life is growing steadily. An
increasing number of people find themselves marginalized, sec-
ond-class citizens unable to control their own destiny and unable
to understand what is happening around them. Racism, powerlessness, solitude, breaking of family and community ties are
new evidences of the marginalization that comes under the category of poverty.

**32. There is also a tragic coincidence that most of the world's
poor have not heard the good news of the gospel of Jesus
Christ; or they could not receive it, because it was not recognized as good news in the way in which it was brought. This
is a double injustice: they are victims of the oppression of an
unjust economic order or an unjust political distribution of
power, and at the same time they are deprived of the knowledge of God's special care for them. To announce the good
news to the poor is to begin to render the justice due to them.**

The church of Jesus Christ is called to preach the good news to the poor following the example of its Lord who was incarnated as poor, who lived as one among them and gave to them the promise of the kingdom of God. Jesus looked at the multitudes with compassion. He recognized the poor as those who were sinned against, victims of both personal and structural sin.

Out of this deep awareness came both his solidarity and his calling to them (Matt. 11:28). His calling was a personalized one. He invited them to come to him, to receive forgiveness of sins and to assume a task. He called them to follow him, because his love incorporated his respect for them as people created by God with freedom to respond. He called them to exercise this responsibility towards God, neighbours and their own lives. **The proclamation of the gospel among the poor is a sign of the messianic kingdom and a priority criterion by which to judge the validity of our missionary engagement today** (appendix 8).

33. This new awareness is an invitation to re-think priorities and life-styles both in the local church and in the worldwide missionary endeavour. Of course, churches and Christians find themselves in very different contexts: some in very wealthy settings where the experience of poverty as it is known to millions in the world today is practically unknown, or in egalitarian societies where the basic needs of life seem to be assured for almost everybody, to situations of extreme poverty. **But the consciousness of the global nature of poverty and exploitation in the world today, the knowledge of the interdependence between nations and the understanding of the international missionary responsibility of the church - all invite, in fact oblige, every church and every Christian to think of ways and means to share the good news with the poor of today.** An objective look at the life of every society, even the most affluent and those which are, theoretically, more just, will show the reality of the poor today in the marginalized, the drop-outs who can-

not cope with modern society, the prisoners of conscience, the dissidents. All of them are waiting for a cup of cold water or for a visit in the name of Christ. **Churches are learning afresh through the poor of the earth to overcome the old dichotomies between evangelism and social action. The "spiritual gospel" and "material gospel" were in Jesus one gospel.**

34. There is no evangelism without solidarity; there is no Christian solidarity that does not involve sharing the knowledge of the kingdom which is God's promise to the poor of the earth. There is here a double credibility test: a proclamation that does not hold forth the promises of the justice of the kingdom to the poor of the earth is a caricature of the gospel; but Christian participation in the struggles for justice which does not point towards the promises of the kingdom also makes a caricature of a Christian understanding of justice.

A growing consensus among Christians today speaks of God's preferential option for the poor.[16] We have there a valid yardstick to apply to our lives as individual Christians, local congregations and as missionary people of God in the world.

35. This concentration point, God's preferential option for the poor, raises the question of the gospel for all those who objectively are not poor or do not consider themselves as such. *It is a clear Christian conviction that God wants all human beings to be saved and to come to the knowledge of truth, but we know that, while God's purpose is for the salvation of all, he has worked historically through the people of Israel and through the incarnation of his own son Jesus Christ. While his purpose is universal, his action is always particular.* What we are learning anew today is that God works through the downtrodden, the persecuted, the poor of the earth. And from there, he is calling all humanity to follow him. "If any one would come after me, let him deny

himself and take up his cross and follow me." (Matt. 16:24)

For all of us, the invitation is clear: to follow Jesus in identification and sharing with the weak, marginalized and
poor of the world, because in them we encounter him.
Knowing from the gospel and from historical experience
that to be rich is to risk forfeiting the kingdom, and knowing how close the links are, in today's world, between the
abundance of some and the needs of others, Christians are
challenged to follow him, surrendering all they are and
have to the kingdom, to a struggle that commits us against
all injustice, against all want. The preferential option for
the poor, instead of discriminating against all other
human beings, is, on the contrary, a guideline for the priorities and behaviour of all Christians everywhere, pointing to the values around which we should organize our
lives and the struggle in which we should put our energy.

36. There is a long experience in the church of voluntarz poverty, people who in obedience to their church calling cast aside all
their belongings, make their own the fate of the poor of the
earth, becoming one of them and living among them. Voluntary
poverty has always been recognized as a source of spiritual
inspiration, of insight into the heart of the gospel.

Today we are gratefully surprised, as churches are growing
among the poor of the earth, by the insight and perspective of
the gospel coming from the communities of the poor. They are
discovering dimensions of the gospel which have long been for-
gotten by the church. The poor of the earth are reading reality
from the other side, from the side of those who do not get the
attention of the history books written by the conquerors, but
who surely get God's attention in the book of life. Living with
the poor and understanding the Bible from their perspective
helps to discover the particular caring with which God both in

the Old and in the New Testament thinks of the marginalized, the downtrodden and the deprived. We realize that the poor to whom Jesus promised the kingdom of God are blessed in their longing for justice and in their hope for liberation. They are both subjects and bearers of the good news; they have the right and the duty to announce the gospel not only among themselves, but also to all other sectors of the human family.

Churches of the poor are spreading the liberating gospel of Jesus Christ in almost every corner of the earth. The richness and freshness of their experience is an inspiration and blessing to churches with a centuries-old history. The centres of the missionary expansion of the church are moving from the North to the South. **God is working through the poor of the earth to awaken the consciousness of humanity to his call for repentance, for justice and for love.**

6. Mission in and to six continents

37. **Everywhere the churches are in missionary situations.** Even in countries where the churches have been active for centuries we see life organized today without reference to Christian values, a growth of secularism understood as the absence of any final meaning. The churches have lost vital contact with the workers and the youth and many others. This situation is so urgent that it commands priority attention of the ecumenical movement. The movement of migrants and political refugees brings the missionary frontier to the doorstep of every parish. **The Christian affirmations on the worldwide missionary responsibility of the church will be credible if they are authenticated by a serious missionary engagement at home.**

As the world becomes smaller, it is possible even for Christians living far away to be aware of and inspired by faithful missionary engagement in a local situation. Of special importance today is the expression of solidarity among the churches crossing political frontiers and the symbolic actions of obedience of one part of the body of Christ that enhance the missionary work of other sectors of the church. So, for example, while programmes related to the elimination of racism may be seen as problems for some churches, such programmes have become, for other churches, a sign of solidarity, an opportunity for witness and a test of Christian authenticity.

Every local congregation needs the awareness of its catholicity which comes from its participation in the mission of the church of Jesus Christ in other parts of the world. Through its witnessing stance in its own situation, its prayers of intercession for churches in other parts of the world, and its sharing of persons and resources, it participates fully in the world mission of the Christian church.

38. This concern for mission everywhere has been tested with the call for a moratorium, a halt - at least for a time - to sending and receiving missionaries and resources across national boundaries, in order to encourage the recovery and affirmation of the identity of every church, the concentration on mission in its own place and the freedom to reconsider traditional relations. The Lausanne Covenant noted that "the reduction of foreign missionaries and money in an evangelized country may sometimes be necessary to facilitate the national church's growth and self-reliance and to release resources for unevangelized areas".[17] Moratorium does not mean the end of the missionary vocation nor of the duty to provide resources for missionary work, but it does mean freedom to reconsider present engagements and to see whether a continuation of what we have been doing for so long is the right style of mission in our day.

Moratorium has to be understood *inside* a concern for world mission. **It is faithfulness of commitment to Christ in each national situation which makes missionary concern in other parts of the world authentic. There can never be a moratorium of mission,**

but it will always be possible, and sometimes necessary, to have a moratorium for the sake of better mission.

39. The story of the churches from their earliest years is the story of faithfulness in their respective localities, but also the story of the carrying of the gospel across national and continental boundaries; first from Jerusalem to Judaea and Samaria, then to Asia Minor, Africa and Europe, now to the ends of the earth. Christians today are the heirs of a long history of those who left their home countries and churches, apostles, monastics, pilgrims, missionaries, emigrants, to work in the name of Jesus Christ, serving and preaching where the gospel had not yet been heard or received. With the European colonization of most of the world and later on with the expansion of the colonial and neo-colonial presence of the Western powers, the churches which had their bases mainly in the West have expanded their missionary service to all corners of the earth.

Surely, many ambiguities have accompanied this development and are present even today, not least the sin of proselytism among other Christian confessions. Churches and missionary organizations are analyzing the experience of these past centuries in order to correct their ways, precisely with the help of the new churches which have come into being in those countries. **The history of the church, the missionary people of God, needs to continue. Each local parish, each Christian, must be challenged to assume responsibility in the total mission of the church. There will always be need for those who have the calling and the gift to cross frontiers, to share the gospel of Jesus Christ and to serve in his name** (appendix 9).

40. Out of this sense of being the whole church in mission, we recognize the specific calling to individuals or communities to commit themselves full time to the service of the church, crossing cultural and national frontiers. **The churches should not allow this specialized calling of the few to be an alibi for the whole church, but rather it should be a symbolic concentra-**

tion of the missionary vocation of the whole church. Looking at the question of people in mission today, "We perceive a change in the direction of mission, arising from our understanding of the Christ who is the centre and who is always in movement towards the periphery. While not in any way denying the continuing significance and necessity of a mutuality between the churches in, the northern and southern hemispheres, we believe that we can discern a development whereby mission in the eighties may increasingly take place within these zones. We feel there will be increasing traffic between the churches of Asia, Africa and Latin America among whose numbers both rich and poor are counted. This development, we expect, will take the form of ever stronger initiatives from the churches of the poor and oppressed at the peripheries. Similarly among the industrialized countries, a new reciprocity, particularly one stemming from the marginalized groups, may lead to sharing at the peripheries of the richer societies. While resources may still flow from financially richer to poorer churches, and while it is not our intention to encourage isolationism, we feel that a benefit of this new reality could well be the loosening of the bond of domination and dependence that still so scandalously characterizes the relationship between many churches of the northern and southern hemispheres respectively."[18]

7. *Witness among people of living faiths*

41. Christians owe the message of God's salvation in Jesus Christ to every person and to every people. Christians make their witness in the context of neighbours who live by other religious convictions and ideological persuasions. **True witness follows Jesus Christ in respecting and affirming the uniqueness and freedom of others.** We confess as Christians that we have often looked for the worst in others and have passed negative judgment upon other religions. We hope as Christians to be learning to witness to our neighbours in a humble, repentant and joyful spirit (appendix 10).

42. The Word is at work in every human life. In Jesus of Nazareth the Word became a human being. The wonder of his ministry of love persuades Christians to testify to people of every religious and non-religious persuasion of this decisive presence of God in Christ. In him is our salvation. Among Christians there are still differences of understanding as to how this salvation in Christ is available to people of diverse religious persuasions. But all agree that witness should be rendered to all.

43. Such an attitude springs from the assurance that God is the Creator of the whole universe and that he has not left himself without witness at any time or any place. **The Spirit of God is constantly at work in ways that pass human understanding and in places that to us are least expected. In entering into a relationship of dialogue with others, therefore, Christians seek to discern the unsearchable riches of God and the way he deals with humanity.** For Christians who come from cultures shaped by another faith, an even more intimate interior dialogue takes place as they seek to establish the connection in their lives between their cultural heritage and the deep convictions of their Christian faith.

44. Christians should use every opportunity to join hands with their neighbours, to work together to be communities of freedom, peace and mutual respect. In some places, state legislation hinders the freedom of conscience and the real exercise of religious freedom. Christian churches as well as communities of other faiths cannot be faithful to their vocation without the freedom and right to maintain their institutional form and confessional identity in a society and to transmit their faith from one generation to another. In those difficult situations, Christians should find a way, along with others, to enter into dialogue with the civil authorities in order to reach a common definition of

religious freedom. With that freedom comes the responsibility to defend through common actions all human rights in those societies (appendix 11).

---

45. Life with people of other faiths and ideologies is an encounter of commitments. Witness cannot be a one-way process, but of necessity is two-way; in it Christians become aware of some of the deepest convictions of their neighbours. It is also the time in which, within a spirit of openness and trust, Christians are able to bear authentic witness, giving an account of their commitment to the Christ, who calls all persons to himself.

Looking Towards the Future

46. Whether among the *secularized masses of industrial societies,* the *emerging new ideologies* around which societies are organized, the resurging religions which people embrace, the *movements of workers and political refugees,* the *people's search for liberation and justice,* the *uncertain pilgrimage of the younger generation* into a future both full of promise and overshadowed by nuclear confrontation - **the church is called to be present and to articulate the meaning of God's love in Jesus Christ for every person and for every situation.**

47. The missionary vocation of the church and its evangelistic calling will not resist the confrontation with the hard realities of daily life if it is not sustained by faith, *a faith supported by prayer, contemplation and adoration.* "Gathering and dispersing, receiving and giving, praise and work, prayer and struggle - this is the true rhythm of Christian engagement in the world."[19] Christians must bring their hearts, minds and wills to the altar of God, knowing that from worship comes wisdom, from prayer comes strength, and from fellowship comes endurance. "To be

incorporated into Christ through the work of the Holy Spirit is the greatest blessing of the kingdom, and the only abiding ground of our missionary activity in the world."[20] **The same Lord who sends his people to cross all frontiers and to enter into the most unknown territories in his name, is the one who assures, "I am with you always, to the close of the age."**

Appendices

1. Now, the gospel was given to the apostles for us by the Lord Jesus Christ; and Jesus the Christ was sent from God. That is to say, Christ received his commission from God, and the apostles theirs from Christ. The order of these two events was in accordance with the will of God. So thereafter, when the apostles had been given their instructions, and all their doubts had been set at rest by the resurrection of our Lord Jesus Christ from the dead, they set out in the full assurance of the Holy Spirit to proclaim the coming of God's kingdom. And as they went through the territories and townships preaching, they appointed their first converts - after testing them by the Spirit - to be bishops and deacons for the believers of the future. (Clement of Rome, *The First Epistle to the Corinthians*, 42, p.45)

2. The difference between Christians and the rest of mankind is not a matter of nationality, or language, or customs. Christians do not live apart in separate cities of their own, speak any special dialect, nor practise any eccentric way of life. The doctrine they profess is not the invention of busy human minds and brains, nor are they, like some, adherents of this or that school of human thought. They pass their lives in whatever township - Greek or foreign - each man's lot has determined; and conform to ordinary local usage in their clothing, diet, and other habits. Nevertheless, the organization of their community does exhibit some features that are remarkable, and even surprising. For instance, though they are residents at home in their own countries, their behaviour there is more like that of transients; they

take their full part as citizens, but they also submit to anything and everything as if they were aliens. For them, any foreign country is a motherland, and any motherland is a foreign country. Like other men, they marry and beget children, though they do not expose their infants. Any Christian is free to share his neighbour's table, but never his marriage-bed. Though destiny has placed them here in the flesh, they do not live after the flesh; their days are passed on the earth, but their citizenship is above in the heavens. They obey the prescribed laws, but in their own private lives they transcend the laws. They show love to all men - and all men persecute them. They are misunderstood, and condemned; yet by suffering death they are quickened into life. They are poor, yet making many rich; lacking all things; yet having all things in abundance. They are dishonoured, yet made glorious in their very dishonour; slandered, yet vindicated. They repay calumny with blessings, and abuse with courtesy. For the good they do, they suffer stripes as evil-doers; and under the strokes they rejoice like men given new life. Jews assail them as heretics, and Greeks harass them with persecutions; and yet of all their ill-wishers there is not one who can produce good grounds for his hostility.

To put it briefly, the relation of Christians to the world is that of a soul to the body... (*The Epistle to Diognetus*, points 5 and 6)

3. There is no single way to witness to Jesus Christ. The church has borne witness in different times and places in different ways. This is important. There are occasions when dynamic action in society is called for; there are others when a word must be spoken; others when the behaviour of Christians one to another is the telling witness. On still other occasions the simple presence of a worshipping community or man is the witness. These different dimensions of witness to the one Lord are always a matter of concrete obedience. To take them in isolation from one another is to distort the gospel. They are inextricably bound together, and together give the true dimensions of evangelism. The important thing is that God's redeeming word be proclaimed and heard. (*Theological Reflection on the Work of Evangelism*, 1959)

4. Through Christ men and women are liberated and empowered with all their energies and possibilities to participate in his messianic work. Through his death on the cross and his resurrection from the dead hope of salvation becomes realistic and reality hopeful. He liberates from the prison of guilt. He takes the inevitability out of history. In him the kingdom of God and of free people is at hand. Faith in Christ releases in man creative freedom for the salvation of the world. He who separates himself from the mission of God separates himself from salvation. (Bangkok Assembly 1973, p.88)

5. Those who take part in the life of Christ and confess him as Lord and Saviour, Liberator and Unifier, are gathered in a community of which the author and sustainer is the Holy Spirit. This communion of the Spirit finds its primary aim and ultimate purpose in the eucharistic celebration and the glorification of the triune God. The doxology is the supreme confession which transcends all our divisions. (*Breaking Barriers*, p.48)

6. As Monseigneur Etchegaray said to the synod a few days ago: "A church which is being renewed in order more effectively to evangelize is a church which is itself willing to be evangelized... We lack not so much the words to say to people as credible persons to say the Word." ("Une église qui se renouvelle pour mieux évangéliser est une église qui accepte d'être évangélisée elle-même... Il nous manque moins de paroles à dire aux hommes que d'hommes-crédibles pour dire la parole.") (Philip Potter's speech to the Roman Catholic synod of bishops, Rome, 1974)

7. There are times and places where the very act of coming together to celebrate the eucharist can be a public witness. In certain states Christians may be discouraged from attending such worship or penalized for it. We hear of those who come together at great risk, and whose courage reveals to those around them how precious is this sacrament. In other situations the eucharist may be an open-air witness so planned that many may see it. Such a joyful celebration as this may offer fresh hope in cynical, secular societies. There is, at the Lord's table, a vision

of God which draws the human heart to the Lord... Each Christian minister and congregation has to seek this understanding, and we can only give some indications: Where a people is being harshly oppressed, the eucharist speaks of the exodus or deliverance from bondage. Where Christians are rejected or imprisoned for their faith, the bread and wine become the life of the Lord who was rejected by men but has become "the chief stone of the corner". Where the church sees a diminishing membership and its budgets are depressing, the eucharist declares that there are no limits to God's giving and no end to hope in him. Where discrimination by race, sex or class is a danger for the community, the eucharist enables people of all sorts to partake of the one food and to be made one people. Where people are affluent and at ease with life, the eucharist says, "As Christ shares his life, share what you have with the hungry." Where a congregation is isolated by politics or war or geography, the eucharist unites us with all God's people in all places and all ages. Where a sister or brother is near death, the eucharist becomes a doorway into the kingdom of our loving Father. (*Your Kingdom Come*, pp.205-206)

8. The proclamation of the gospel to the poor is a sign of the new age inaugurated by Jesus Christ. As witnessed in the scriptures, the situation of the poor, and what the Holy Spirit can do among them, is a wonderful locus for the manifestation of God's love and power. This implies that evangelization to the poor, with the poor, for and by the poor, must be considered one of the churches' highest priorities. (*Towards a Church in Solidarity with the Poor*, p.26)

9. The proclamation of the good news is a continual necessity and all people, believers and unbelievers, are challenged to hear and respond since conversion is never finished. We acknowledge and gladly accept our special obligation to those who have never heard the good news of the kingdom. New frontiers are continually being discovered. Jesus our Lord is always ahead of us and draws us to follow him, often in unexpected ways. The

Christian community is a community on the way, making its proclamation, both to itself and to chose beyond its fellowship, even as it shows forth its other marks "on the way". (*Your Kingdom Come*, p.195)

10. Christians engaged in faithful "dialogue in community" with people of other faiths and ideologies cannot avoid asking themselves penetrating questions about the place of these people in the activity of God in history. They ask these questions not in theory, but in terms of what God may be doing in the lives of purposes or in ways prejudicial to the self-understanding of Christians and others;hundreds of millions of men and women who live in and seek community together with Christians, but along different ways. So dialogue should proceed in terms of people of other faiths and ideologies rather than of theoretical, impersonal systems. This is not to deny the importance of religious traditions and their inter-relationships but it is vital to examine how faiths and ideologies have given direction to the daily living of individuals and groups and actually affect dialogue on both sides.

Approaching the theological questions in this spirit Christians should proceed...

- with repentance, because they know how easily they m i s - construe God's revelation in Jesus Christ, betraying it in their actions and posturing as the owners of God's truth rather than, as in fact they are, the undeserving recipients of grace;

- with humility, because they so often perceive in people of other faiths and ideologies a spirituality, dedication, compassion and a wisdom which should forbid them making judgments about others as though from a position of superiority; in particular they should avoid using ideas such as "anonymous Christians", "the Christian presence", "the unknown Christ", in ways not intended by those who proposed them for theological purposes or in waysprejudicial to the self-understanding of Christians and others;

- with joy, because it is not themselves they preach, it is Jesus Christ, perceived by many people of living faiths and ideologies as prophet, holy one, teacher, example; but confessed byChristians as Lord and Saviour, himself the faithful witness and the coming one (Rev. 1:5-7);

- with integrity, because they do not enter into dialogue with others except in this penitent and humble joyfulness in the Lord Jesus Christ, making clear to others their own experience and witness, even as they seek to hear from others their expressions of deepest conviction and insight. All these would mean an openness and exposure, the capacity to be wounded which we see in the example of our Lord Jesus Christ and which we sum up in the word vulnerability. (*Guidelines on Dialogue with People of Living Faiths and Ideologies*, pp.11-12)

11. The attitude of the churches to the ongoing revivals or reassertions of institutional religions will have to vary according to the specific situation. In some countries the situation of the churches has become extremely difficult, particularly where the revival has led to erosion of civil liberties including, in some cases, the freedom of religion.

The prayer of the worldwide church must be that the Christians in those situations may find strength in the Holy Spirit to witness for the kingdom of God in humility and endurance, that oppression can be met with love and that God may use their sufferings to bring about a renewal of their own Christian faith.

We express our solidarity with them as with all oppressed people.

In all situations of religious conflicts the churches are called upon to help their individual members to re-examine their own basic loyalties and to understand better their neighbours of other faiths. On all accounts, the churches must try to find meeting points in their contexts for dialogue and cooperation with people of other faiths. The above-mentioned criteria as well as the common cultural heritage and a commitment to national unity and development could be the starting points for a mutual witness in dialogue. This presupposes a mind of openness, respect and truthfulness in the churches and among their members towards neighbours of other faiths but also courage to give an account of the hope we have in Jesus Christ as our Lord.

As has been pointed out in the Guidelines on Dialogue, received by the central committee of the WCC, Jamaica 1979, a dialogical approach to neighbours of other faiths and convictions is not in contradiction with mission. Our mission to witness to Jesus Christ can never be given up. The proclamation of the gospel to the whole world remains an urgent obligation for all Christians and it should be carried out in the spirit of our Lord, not in a crusading and aggressive spirit.

"Let us behave wisely towards those outside our number; let us use the opportunity to the full. Let our conversation be always full of grace and never insipid; let us study how best to talk with each person we meet" (Col. 4:5-6). (*Your Kingdom Come*, pp.187-88)

---

1 Philip Potter's speech to the Roman Catholic Synod of Bishops, Rome, 1974.

2 Constitution of the World Council of Churches.

3 Constitution of the Conference on World Mission and Evangelism.

4 *Your Kingdom Come*, p. 210.

5 *Your Kingdom Come*, p. 196.

6 "Confessing Christ Today, Reports of Groups at a Consultation of Orthodox Theologians", p. 8.

7 *Breaking Barriers*, p. 233.

8 *Confessing Christ Today*, op. cit., pp.10 and 3.

9 *Breaking Barriers*, p.48.

10 Philip Potter, *op. cit.*

11 *Your Kingdom Come*, p.206.

12 Common witness, p.28.

13 *Ibid.*

14 SEDOS bulletin 81/no. 7.

15 *Breaking Barriers,* p.46.

16 Catholic Bishops Conference, Puebla, 1979, para. 1134.

17 Lausanne Covenant, no. 9.

18 *Your Kingdom Come*, pp. 220/221.

19 *Your Kingdom Come*, p.205.

20 *Your Kingdom Come*, p.204.

Towards Common Witness: A Call to Adopt Responsible Relationships in Mission and to Renounce Proselytism

Presentation

It is highly significant that the call for a further WCC study or update on proselytism and common witness was made when the central committee met in Moscow in 1989, the year during which the Berlin wall was to fall, with all the consequences in shaping new political realities in the world. There is no need for a long presentation, in this case, since the preface and the introduction originally published with the document give sufficient information as to its purpose, history and status. It is, however, important to note that this document was commended by the 1997 central committee to the churches for reflection and action. It must also be said that the call to renounce proselytism does not in any way negate the strong declarations of the 1982 Ecumenical Affirmation on the necessity for a clear witness to the name of Jesus Christ. Proselytism in the sense it is understood in WCC documents is considered a betrayal of authentic evangelism. To renounce proselytism does not mean to renounce evangelism. The difference between abusive proselytism and authentic evangelism is similar to that between the mission strategy refused by Jesus in the temptation story (Matt. 4:1-11) and the one promoted by the resurrected Christ in the great commission (Matt. 28:16-20).

The 1997 document reaffirms the conviction that mission in unity is a key test of mutual respect by churches. "Authentic common witness presupposes respect for and understanding of other traditions and confessions."[1] The recommendations which are part of the document and were also agreed to by the central committee mention several matters which gained even more importance since 1997. One of them is the call for further study on ecclesiology and mission. As other similar international dialogues also showed, common witness - which normally should include evangelism - is hindered if there is not at least a basic recognition of elements of authentic Christian faith and of the true church in the mission partner.[2]

In its very short first chapter on the mission imperative, the 1997 statement makes clear reference to the concept of missio Dei, one of the important elements of an ecumenical missiology, present in the 1982 Ecumenical Affirmation but more indirectly because of the preferred use of the kingdom of God terminology in that document. Towards Common Witness also quotes one of the most famous sentences coming from the WCC Canberra assembly, describing the vision of mission in unity as follows:

> A reconciled humanity and renewed creation (cf. Eph. 1:9-10) is the goal of the mission of the church. The vision of God uniting all things in Christ is the driving force of its life and sharing.[3]

The combination of a missio Dei theology with the theme of reconciliation appeared shortly after the world mission conference in San Antonio (1989) in the preparation for the Canberra assembly. It proved a helpful impulse and represented a foretaste of the core of ecumenical missiology in the first decade of the new millennium.[4]

If the WCC has any reason for existence, calling the churches to manifest the unity given by Christ and for which he died, it must stand firm on the question of common witness or mission in unity and challenge any form of proselytism as defined in this document . [5]

JM

1 *Towards Common Witness*, see p. 47.

2 The recommendations are on pp. 56-57. For a subsequent study on ecclesiology and mission, cf. *IRM* vol. 90, no. 358, July 2001, and no. 359, Oct. 2001 and the study process on ecclesiology by Faith and Order. Cf. also the affirmations made during the international dialogue between Pentecostals and Roman Catholics, started in 1972, of which the fourth phase was on evangelization, proselytism and common witness (1990-97): "The members of the dialogue observed that proselytism exists, in large parts, because Pentecostals and Catholics do not have a common understanding of the church", "Pentecostal-Roman Catholic Dialogue; Evangelization, Proselytism and Common Witness", §69, in Jeffrey Gros et al. eds, *Growth in Agreement II: Reports and Agreed Statements of Ecumenical Conversations on a World Level, 1982-1998*, WCC, 2000, p.765.

3 *Towards Common Witness*, see p.46. Today, this would probably be formulated in a slightly different way, in the sense that the reconciled humanity and renewed creation is the goal of God's own overall mission, in which the church participates by pointing to and signifying that hope and divine reality.

4 One of the recommendations of the 1997 document relates to reconciliation: "promote efforts towards reconciliation by addressing historical wounds and bitter memories". The missiological reflection pursued since 1997 emphasized what is meant by reconciliation processes and healing of memories and its essential contribution to the search for church unity.

5 In the mid-1990s, the WCC also conducted a study on international relationships in mission, which follows the same idea of mission in unity, analyzing its consequence at the worldwide level for relationships between churches of different regions and cultures. The results were published in *IRM* vol. 86, no. 342, July 1997.

Towards Common Witness: A Call to Adopt Responsible Relationships in Mission and to Renounce Proselytism

Preface

Within the ecumenical movement and the World Council of Churches the concern for common witness and the unity of the churches has always been a priority, and proselytism has been recognized as a scandal and counter-witness. Ecumenical statements have repeatedly expressed the need for the clearer practice of responsible relationships in mission, a sharper commitment to witness in unity, and renunciation of all forms of proselytism. Yet during these almost fifty years of ecumenical fellowship in the WCC, proselytism has continued to be a painful reality in the life of the churches.[1]

The issue of proselytism is again being raised as a major factor dividing the churches and a threat to the ecumenical movement itself. In the face of such a complex situation, the central committee in Moscow, 1989, requested the former Commission on World Mission and Evangelism to "take up this issue [of proselytism] for further study and action, examining also the existing statements for up-dating if necessary". A similar request was made by the fifth world conference on Faith and Order (Santiago de Compostela, 1993), which asked for a "new and broader study of mission, evangelism and proselytism".

The present document, which has been elaborated by Programme Unit II, is in response to these requests. In order to reflect accurately on current realities and find appropriate ways forward, the Unit embarked on a broad consultative study process. Mission agencies, churches, missiologists and theologians, local congregations and monastic orders in different parts of the world participated by correspondence. Furthermore a series of consultations was organized: "Towards Responsible

Relationships in Mission" (Chambésy, 1993); an Orthodox consultation on "Mission and Proselytism" (Sergiev Possad, Russia, 1995); "Called to Common Witness" (Manila, 1995); and "Common Witness" (Bossey, 1996). Special efforts were made to bring together in dialogue the "proselytizers" and "proselytized" and to involve not only WCC member churches but members of the evangelical, Pentecostal and charismatic constituencies.

Documents and statements on this issue from churches and other organizations have been carefully studied and analyzed and their insights incorporated in the present statement. Permanent contact has been maintained with the Joint Working Group in a spirit of mutual cooperation and sharing. Its study document, "The Challenge of Proselytism and the Calling to Common Witness" (1995), was one of the basic texts used in the elaboration of this statement. The Unit II study, however, was undertaken with much broader participation, and emphasizes the missiological and pastoral implications of proselytism in the life of local churches on the way towards common witness and Christian unity. An earlier draft of this statement was used as a resource paper at the conference on world mission and evangelism in Salvador, Brazil (1996).

This statement is presented in the conviction that it is both timely and important for churches in all parts of the world. Its genesis also reflects the spirit of the WCC's "Common Understanding and Vision" document, in that it has provided space for wider participation in ecumenical discussions.

September 1997

> **The aims of this statement are: (1) to make churches and Christians aware of the bitter reality of proselytism today; (2) to call those involved in proselytism to recognize its disastrous effects on church unity, relationships among Christians and the credibility of the gospel and, therefore, to renounce it; and (3) to encourage the churches and mission agencies to avoid all forms of competition in mission and to commit themselves anew to witness in unity.**

Introduction

Developments in different parts of the world in recent years have compelled the ecumenical family to re-examine issues related to common witness and proselytism in greater depth. For the WCC the situation is made even more urgent by the fact that complaints of proselytistic activities are being made against some of its own member churches as well as churches and groups outside its fellowship.

Among present-day realities damaging the relationships between churches in different parts of the world and thus requiring the urgent attention of the ecumenical family are:

- competitive missionary activities, especially in Central and Eastern Europe, Africa, Asia and Latin America, carried out independently by foreign missionary groups, churches and individuals, often directed at people already belonging and committed to one of the churches in those countries, and often leading to the establishment of parallel ecclesial structures;

- the re-emergence of tensions between the Orthodox and the Roman Catholic Church concerning the Eastern Rite Catholic churches; [2]

- a sharp increase in the number of new mission agencies based in the South working independently in other parts of the world, often without contact with the churches in those countries;

- growing frustration among churches, especially in the South, whose members are being lured to other churches by offers of humanitarian aid;

- the humanitarian work done among immigrants, poor, lonely and uprooted people in big cities intended to influence them to change their denominational allegiance;

- the growth of religious fundamentalism and intolerance;

- the growing impact of sects and new religious movements in many parts of the world;

- the discrediting of established minority Christian churches in multifaith communities.

The aims of this statement are: (1) to make churches and Christians aware of the bitter reality of proselytism today; (2) to call those involved in proselytism to recognize its disastrous effects on church unity, relationships among Christians and the credibility of the gospel and, therefore, to renounce it; and (3) to encourage the churches and mission agencies to avoid all forms of competition in mission and to commit themselves anew to witness in unity.

Christian Witness and Religious Freedom

1. The mission imperative

Christian mission is primarily and ultimately God's mission - the *missio Dei*. It is centred in the loving and eternal purpose of the triune God for humankind and all of creation, revealed in Jesus Christ. Central to God's mission is the life-giving presence of the Holy Spirit, who continues the mission of Christ through the church and remains the source of its missionary dynamism. The

WCC Canberra assembly (1991) described a vision of mission-in unity: "A reconciled humanity and renewed creation (cf. Eph. 1:9-10) is the goal of the mission of the church. The vision of God uniting all things in Christ is the driving force of its life and sharing."[3]

As the body of Christ, constituted, sustained and energized by the life-giving presence of the Holy Spirit, the church is missionary by nature. It proclaims that in Jesus Christ the incarnate Word, who died and rose from the dead, salvation is offered to all as God's gift of love, mercy and liberation.

Participating in God's mission is an imperative for all Christians and all churches, not only for particular individuals or specialized groups. It is an inner compulsion, rooted in the profound demands of Christ's love, to invite others to share in the fullness of life Jesus came to bring (cf. John 10:10).

Mission in Christ's way is *holistic,* for the whole person and the totality of life are inseparable in God's plan of salvation accomplished in Jesus Christ. It is *local* - "the primary responsibility for mission, where there is a local church, is with that church in its own place". It is also *universal*, that is, to all peoples, beyond all frontiers of race, caste, gender, culture, nation - to "the ends of the earth" in every sense (cf. Acts 1:8; Mark 16:15; Luke 24:47).

> **"The primary responsibility for mission, where there is a local church, is with that church in its own place."**

2. Common witness: mission in unity

Numerous WCC documents have recalled the intrinsic relation between the credibility of the mission of the church in the world and the unity among Christians - underscored in the prayer of Jesus "that they all may be one... so that the world may believe" (John 17:21) and historically realized among the apostles in Jerusalem already on the day of Pentecost. Common witness is "the witness that the churches, even while separated, bear together, especially through joint efforts, by manifesting whatever divine gifts of truth and life they already share and experience in common".[5] It may be thought of as "a 'eucharistic vision of life' which gives thanks for what God has done, is doing, and will do for the salvation of the world through acts of joyous self-offering". [6]

Common witness is "the witness that the churches, even while separated, bear together, especially through joint efforts, by manifesting whatever divine gifts of truth and life they already share and experience in common".

Despite the many barriers which keep the churches apart, the WCC member churches have been able to recognize a certain degree of ecclesial communion among themselves, imperfect though that may yet be. Confessing "the Lord Jesus Christ as God and Saviour according to the scriptures", they seek through the WCC to "fulfil together their common calling to the glory of one God, Father, Son and Holy Spirit".[7] On this basis, other grounds for common witness to the whole world can be affirmed together. Mutual recognition of baptism (as expressed in the WCC's Baptism, Eucharist and Ministry text) is the foundation for Christian unity and common witness.

Authentic common witness presupposes respect and understanding for other traditions and confessions.

Authentic common witness presupposes respect and understanding for other traditions and confessions. What should be emphasized is that which is common and can be done together, rather than the barriers which separate. Even when apparently irreconcilable differences remain on certain issues, the truth should be spoken in love (Eph. 4:15), for the building up of the irreconcilable differences remain on certain issues, the truth should be spoken in love (Eph. 4:15), for the building up of the church (Eph.4:12), rather than for giving prominence to one's position over against that of others. There is more that unites the churches than separates them. These unifying elements should be looked for in building up witness in unity.

3. Mission in the context of religious freedom

God's truth and love are given freely and call for a free response. Free will is one of the major gifts with which God has entrusted humans. God does not force anyone to accept God's revelation and does not save anyone by force. On the basis of this notion, the International Missionary Council and the World Council of Churches (in process of formation) developed a definition of religious freedom as a fundamental human right. This definition was adopted by the WCC first assembly in Amsterdam (1948), and at the suggestion of the WCC's Commission of the Churches on International Affairs it was subsequently incorporated in the Universal Declaration of Human Rights: "Everyone has the right to freedom of thought, conscience and religion. This right includes the freedom to change his/her religion or belief, and freedom, either alone or in community with others, in public or in private, to manifest his/her religion or belief, in teaching, practice, worship and observance." The same principle is to be applied in mission work.

The WCC fifth assembly (1975) reaffirmed the centrality of religious liberty, stating that "the right to religious freedom has been and continues to be a major concern of member churches and the WCC. However this right should never be seen as belonging exclusively to the church... This right is inseparable from other fundamental human rights. No religious community should plead for its own religious liberty without active respect and reverence for the faith and basic rights of others. Religious liberty should never be used to claim privileges. For the church this right is essential so that it can fulfil its responsibilities which arise out of the Christian faith. Central to these responsibilities is the obligation to serve the whole community."[8] One's own freedom must always respect, affirm and promote the freedom of others; it must not contravene the golden rule: "In everything do to others as you would have them do to you" (Matt. 7:12).

Proselytism - A Counterwitness

While the word "proselyte" was originally used to designate a person who became a member of the Jewish community by believing in Yahweh and respecting the Law of Moses, and subsequently, in early Christian times, for a person of another faith who converted to Christianity, proselytism in later centuries took on a negative connotation due to changes in the content, motivation, spirit and methods of "evangelism".

"Proselytism" is now used to mean the encouragement of Christians who belong to a church to change their denominational allegiance, through ways and means that "contradict the spirit of Christian love, violate the freedom of the human person and diminish trust in the Christian witness of the church".[9]

Proselytism is "the corruption of witness".[10] On the surface, proselytism may appear as genuine and enthusiastic missionary activity; and some people involved in it are genuinely committed Christians who believe that they are doing mission in Christ's way. It is the aim, spirit and methodology of this activity which make it proselytism.

Some of the characteristics which clearly distinguish proselytism from authentic Christian witness are:

- unfair criticism or caricaturing of the doctrines, beliefs and practices of another church without attempting to understand or enter into dialogue on those issues; some who venerate icons are accused of worshipping idols; others are ridiculed for alleged idolatry towards Mary and the saints or denounced for praying for the dead;

- presenting one's church or confession as "the *true* church" and its teachings as "the *right* faith" and the only way to salvation, rejecting baptism in other churches as invalid and persuading people to be rebaptized;.

- portraying one's own church as having high moral and spiritual status over against the perceived weaknesses and problems of other churches;

- taking advantage of and using unfaithfully the problems which may arise in another church for winning new members for one's own church;

- offering humanitarian aid or educational opportunities as an inducement to join another church;

- using political, economic, cultural and ethnic pressure or historical arguments to win others to one's own church;

- taking advantage of lack of education or Christian instruction which makes people vulnerable to changing their church allegiance;

- using physical violence or moral and psychological pressure to induce people to change their church affiliation: this includes the use of media techniques profiling a particular church in a way that excludes, disparages or stigmatizes its adherents, harassment through repeated house calls, material and spiritual threats, and insistence on the "superior" way to salvation offered by a particular church;

- exploiting people's loneliness, illness, distress or even disillusionment with their own church in order to "convert" them.

Common witness is constructive: it enriches, challenges, strengthens and builds up solid Christian relationships and fellowship. Through word and deed, it makes the gospel relevant to the contemporary world. Proselytism is a perversion of

> **Common witness is constructive: it enriches, challenges, strengthens and builds up solid Christian relationships and fellowship.**

authentic Christian witness and thus a counterwitness. It does not build up but destroys. It brings about tensions, scandal and division, and is thus a destabilizing factor for the witness of the church of Christ in the world. It is always a wounding of koinonia, creating not fellowship but antagonistic parties.

Nevertheless, it must be acknowledged that some people may move from one church to another out of true and genuine conviction, without any proselytistic pressure or manipulation, as a free decision in response to their experience of the life and witness of another church.

The churches must continually assess their own internal life to see whether some of the reasons people change church allegiance may lie with the churches themselves.

Guidelines for Responsible Relationships in Mission

1. Issues for further study and reflection

Growth towards responsible relationships in mission which promote genuine Christian common witness and avoid proselytism will require further dialogue, reflection and study in a number of important ecclesiological, theological and other areas:

- historical and social factors, including (1) diversity of experience among different churches, (2) unawareness or different understandings of the history of one's own church and other churches, leading to wounded memories, and (3) dissimilar perspectives and perceptions among majority and minority churches in contexts where a single church has come to be identified with a given nation, people or culture;

- different and even contradictory understandings of the content of Christian faith - regarding worship, sacraments and the teaching authority of the church - and of the limits of legitimate diversity in these areas;

- different understandings of the nature of an individual's church membership and Christian commitment, particularly reflected in the use of expressions conveying value judgments (such as "nominal", "committed", "true" or "born-again Christian", "unchurched", "evangelization" and "re-evangelization"), which are often a source of tension among the churches, leading to accusations of proselytism;

- different understandings of the aim of mission, leading to differences in ethos and style of mission, particularly around those concepts of "church growth" and "church expansion" which seem to give priority to the number of "converts" and thus seem to encourage mission among those who are already members of a Christian church;

- different understandings of the universality of mission, particularly around the validity of the early Christian principle of "canonical territory", according to which the local church already present in any place is primarily responsible for the Christian life of the people there and no other Christian individual, group or church may act or establish ecclesial structures without consulting and cooperating with the local church.

2. The way forward: practical proposals

Despite the problems still to be overcome, ecumenical reflection and experience in the last few decades have demonstrated that reconciliation and mutual understanding are possible and that witness in unity can become a reality on an even greater scale.

As new contexts call for new initiatives in proclaiming the gospel in unity, churches in partnership in mission must commit themselves to:

- deepened understanding of what it means to be church in today's world, and acceptance and celebration of their inter-relatedness in the one body of Christ (cf. 1 Cor. 12:12);

- deepened conviction that it is God's mission in which the churches share as God's co-workers, not their own;

- efforts to come to a greater common understanding and vision of their missionary role in contemporary society;

- reaching out together in Christ's way to new frontiers of mission - listening, accompanying, walking with, resourcing, receiving from one another;

- renewed determination to manifest together "the one hope of [their] calling" (Eph. 4:4) in order to share more fully in the divine plan of salvation for the reconciliation and gathering up of all peoples and all things in Christ (cf. Eph. 1:9-10).

> **"We decry the practice of those who carry out their endeavours in mission and evangelism in ways which destroy the unity of the body of Christ, human dignity and the very lives and cultures of those being 'evangelized'; we call on them to confess their participation in and to renounce proselytism."**

Because the way to evangelizing in ecumenical fellowship and partnership is still long, churches in partnership in mission must:

- repent of past failures and reflect more self-critically on their ways of relating to one another and their methods of evangelizing, in order to overcome anything in their the-ological or doctrinal expressions or missionary policies and strategies which shows lack of love, understanding and trust of other churches;

- renounce all forms of denominational competition and rivalry and the temptation to proselytize members of other Christian traditions as contrary to Jesus' prayer for the unity of his disciples (John 17:21);

- avoid establishing parallel ecclesial structures, but rather stimulate, help and cooperate with the existing local churches in their evangelistic work in society at large as well as in relation to their own people, especially so-called nominal members;

- condemn any manipulation of humanitarian assistance to individual Christians or churches to induce people into changing their denominational allegiance or to further the missionary goals of one church at the expense of another;

- help people who are in process of changing their church allegiance to discern whether they are being guided by worthy or unworthy motives (such as social advancement or better life opportunities);

- learn to "speak the truth in love" to one another when they consider others to be proselytizing or engaging in dishonest practices in evangelism.

This Christian fellowship and partnership will not be possible unless Christians and churches:

- listen to one another in genuine dialogue aimed at overcoming ignorance, prejudices or misunderstandings, understanding their differences in the perspective of Christian unity and avoiding unjust accusations, polemics, disparagement and rejection;

- ensure greater sharing of information and accountability in mission at all levels, including prior discussion before launching programmes for evangelism;

- encourage, strengthen and complement one another in missionary activity in an ecumenical spirit, including prior consultation with the church in an area to see what are the possibilities of missionary collaboration and witness in unity;

- demonstrate willingness to learn from others - for example, from their dynamism, enthusiasm and joy in mission, their sense of community, their rejoicing in the Spirit, their spirituality;

- make greater efforts for inner renewal in their own traditions and cultural contexts.

Conclusion

With the Salvador world mission conference,"we decry the practice of those who carry out their endeavours in mission and evangelism in ways which destroy the unity of the body of Christ, human dignity and the very lives and cultures of those being 'evangelized'; we call on them to confess their participation in and to renounce proselytism".[11]

Called to one hope, we commit ourselves to our common call to mission and to work towards mission in unity. We actively seek a new era of "mission in Christ's way" at the dawn of the third millennium, enriched by one another's gifts and bound together in the Holy Spirit.

As you, Father, are in me and I am in you, may they also be in us, so that the world may believe that you have sent me. The glory that you have given me I have given them, so that they may be one, as we are one, I in them and you in me, that they may become completely one, so that the world may know that you have sent me and have loved them even as you have loved me (John 17:20-23).

> **Called to one hope, we commit ourselves to our common call to mission and to work towards mission in unity. We actively seek a new era of "mission in Christ's way" at the dawn of the third millennium, enriched by one another's gifts and bound together in the Holy Spirit.**

Reccommendations

In addition to commending the document "Towards Common Witness" to the churches for their reflection and action, the Central Committee approved the following recommendations to facilitate the implementation of the document:

1. That the churches and related agencies:

- make greater efforts to educate their own faithful in local congregations, Sunday schools, training centres and seminaries to respect and love members of other churches as sisters and brothers in Christ;

- actively promote knowledge of the heritages and contributions of other churches that, despite differences, confess the same Jesus Christ as God and Saviour, worship the same triune God and are engaged in the same witness in the world;

- promote efforts towards reconciliation by addressing historical wounds and bitter memories;

- initiate (with the assistance of the WCC when necessary) encounter and dialogue at the local, national and regional levels with those engaging in mission work that is perceived as proselytism, in order to help them understand their motivations, make them aware of the negative impact of their activities, and promote responsible relationships in mission;

- seek opportunities for working together with other churches on pastoral and social issues that affect local communities and countries as a whole, and be open to authentic cooperation with others in addressing the needs of the people being served;

- together renounce proselytism as a denial of authentic witness and an obstruction to the unity of the church, and urge support for common witness, unity and understanding among the churches proclaiming the gospel;

- continue to pray together for Christian unity, allowing God's Spirit to lead the churches into fuller truth and faithfulness.

2. *That the World Council of Churches:*

strengthen its emphasis on ecumenical formation using all resources of its education sector, in view of the growing trend towards confessionalism and confessional rivalries;

undertake a study on ecclesiology and mission, since many of the points of tension and division in relation to common witness stem from conflicting understandings in these areas.

Although it is recognized that the main responsibility for implementing the "Towards Common Witness" document lies with the churches, the WCC should play a facilitating role in stimulating the dialogue within and among the churches.

1 In fact, concern about proselytism as an ecumenical issue antedates the establishment of the WCC. The 1920 encyclical of the Ecumenical Patriarchate, which proposed the foundation of a "koinonia" of churches, asked for the cessation of proselytizing activities. In the preliminary Faith and Order and Life and Work meetings which took place in the same year the issue of proselytism was again raised. Since the very establishment of the WCC the issue of proselytism has been identified as one of the hindrances to Christian unity. As early as 1954, the central committee in Evanston decided that in view of difficulties which were affecting relationships between WCC member churches, a commission should be appointed to study further the issue of proselytism and religious liberty. After a number of years of labourious study, a statement on "Christian Witness, Proselytism and Religious Liberty in the Setting of the World Council of Churches", drafted by the commission and revised twice by the central committee (1956 and 1960), was received by the WCC third assembly (New Delhi, 1961).

Issues of proselytism and common witness have also been on the agenda of the Joint Working Group between the Roman Catholic Church and the World Council of Churches, which has elaborated three important study documents: "Common Witness and Proselytism" (1970); "Common Witness" (1982); and "The Challenge of Proselytism and the Calling to Common Witness" (1995). Furthermore, many documents and declarations on the issue of common witness and proselytism have been produced recently by local and international bilateral dialogues between churches. Studies have also been done by the Conference of European Churches and the Middle East Council of Churches.

2 The Eastern Rite Catholic churches originated in those groups of former Orthodox who entered into full communion with the Roman Catholic Church around the bishop of Rome, while retaining various Eastern liturgical and canonical traditions inherited from their mother churches.

3 *Signs of the Spirit: Official Report of the Seventh Assembly*, Michael Kinnamon ed., WCC, 1991, p.100.

4 *Called to One Hope: The Gospel in Diverse Cultures*, Christopher Duraisingh ed., WCC, 1998, p.72.

5 Thomas Stransky, "*Common Witness*", in *Dictionary of the Ecumenical Movement*, Nicholas Lossky et al. eds, WCC, 1991, p.197.

6 *On the Way to Fuller Koinonia: Official Report of the Fifth World Conference on Faith and Order*, Santiago de Compostela, 1993, Thomas F. Best and Günther Gassmann eds, WCC, 1994, p.254.

7 WCC "Basis", from "Constitution and Rules of the World Council of Churches".

8 Cf. *Breaking Barriers: Official Report of the Fifth Assembly of the World Council of Churches*, Nairobi, David M. Paton ed., Grand Rapids MI, Eerdmans, 1976, p.106. Cf. also the report of the Orthodox consultation on "Mission and Proselytism", Sergiev Possad, Russia, 1995.

9 Cf. report of the Sergiev Possad consultation on "Mission and Proselytism".

10 "Revised Report on 'Christian Witness, Proselytism and Religious Liberty in the Setting of the World Council of Churches'", in *Minutes and Reports of the Central Committee of the World Council of Churches*, St Andrews, Scotland, August 1960, WCC, 1960, p.214.

11 *Called to One Hope*, pp.74-75.

Mission and Evangelism in Unity Today

Presentation

This document has not been presented to any governing body of the World Council of Churches, and so has less "official" status than the first two published in this book. Its own origin and history are briefly summarized in the first paragraphs. Whereas there had been some intention to revise the 1982 Ecumenical Affirmation in the early 1990s, consultations with mission theologians and boards, and with churches and the constituency led the WCC and its department responsible for mission work between the Canberra and Harare assemblies to abandon the idea and move to the production of a statement which would summarize new insights, emphases and trends since 1982, allowing the Affirmation its unique status as the main official WCC document on mission.

A first draft of the document was discussed at the world mission conference in Salvador da Bahía, Brazil, in 1996, during which it became clear that the paper needed fundamental revision. A new start was made in the years following Salvador, and the revised statement was presented to one of the padare workshops held during the 1998 assembly in Harare. One and a half years later, the document was presented together with a summary of the reactions collected during the assembly to the new Commission on World Mission and Evangelism (CWME Commission)[1] at its first meeting in Morges, Switzerland, in the year 2000. The CWME Commission adopted the statement as a study document to be used for reflection and dialogue on mission in preparation for the next world mission conference in 2005.

The definitions given to "mission" and "evangelism"[2] are worth noting, because they formulate in explicit terms what earlier texts merely imply. Whereas many people would not express their understanding exactly in the same words, these are the definitions mostly used in WCC circles.[3]

The document clearly refers to missio Dei as the overarching frame for understanding Christian mission. It develops it in reference to God as Father, Son and Holy Spirit, thus strengthening the move from an exclusively Christocentric interpretation of mission to a trinitarian one. But the text does not deviate from the usual ecumenical consensus when it emphasizes the specificity of the Spirit's role in mission without separating the Spirit's work from Christ.[4]

The document also attempts to summarize how missiologists connected to the WCC understand and interpret trends in economic, political and social life since 1989, as well as developments in church life. This provides the background for interpret

ing the document's focus on fullness of life as a key term for understanding what God's mission is all about, and on the call to life in community, reflecting something of God's own community of three-in-one.[5] The two following chapters do not bring new theological insights, but are an attempt at summarizing the results of the world mission conferences held since the publication of the Ecumenical Affirmation, i.e. San Antonio (1989) and Salvador (1996), with an emphasis on two major items not treated extensively in the Ecumenical Affirmation: the relation between gospel and cultures,[6] and a missiological approach to the relation between Christian faith and other religions.[7]

The long chapter on mission in unity refers to the 1997 document on common witness, and extends its scope to the matter of the sharing of power and resources in worldwide mission work and structures. The closing sentences are remarkable: those clear formulations of ecumenical convictions and commitments[8] can be read as a summary of ecumenical mission theology at the beginning of the second millennium.

With this document, the CWME commission established the basis for the content of the next world mission conference.

JM

1 The CWME Commission has existed since 1961, but its name and function was changed after the Canberra assembly in 1991, when it was integrated into the Unit II Commission. In Harare 1998, it was re-established as CWME.

2 *Mission and Evangelism in Unity Today*, §7.

3 This may be true in theory and at world level. It must be said, however, that in specific contexts, one of these terms is loaded with such negative memories that it cannot be used. Sometimes that is true for both terms ("mission" and "evangelism"), and then one has to refer to "witness". Other persons linked to WCC mission networks use both terms interchangeably and do not wish to distinguish between them. It is important, however, to be as clear as possible about use of terminology. In some Roman Catholic texts, e.g., the term evangelization is preferred for overall holistic witness, while "mission" relates to the specific ministry of cross-cultural missions, to the witness to people who do not yet know Christ (*missio ad gentes*).

4 §12. This is in line with the commentary published by Faith and Order on the Nicene Creed in 1991. Cf. *Confessing the One Faith: An Ecumenical Explication of the Apostolic Faith as It Is Confessed in the Nicene-Constantinopolitan Creed* (381),new rev. version, WCC, 1991, F&O Paper no. 153, p.78.

5 Since the 1980 Melbourne conference (section III), there has been a growing emphasis on the importance of community in WCC mission conferences. In San Antonio, 1989, this was discussed in section IV, and in Salvador, in section III mainly. This trend increased in the years following the adoption of *Mission and Evangelism in Unity Today*.

6 Inculturation or contextualization featured at the 1972-73 world mission conference in Bangkok with its emphasis on cultural identity. It was only during the study process on gospel and cultures, which prepared the main content of the Salvador conferences in 1996, that the question was taken up again and in a fresh way in WCC's missiology. main content of the Salvador conference in 1996, that the question was taken up again and in a fresh way in WCC's missiology.

7 The milestone on this question is to be found in the report of section I of the San Antonio conference with an affirmation that still reflects ecumenical consensus on this difficult question, cf. §58 of *Mission and Evangelism in Unity Today*.

8 §§76 and 77.

Mission and Evangelism in Unity Today

Introduction

1. The ecumenical movement has its origins in the missionary movement, for the contemporary search for the unity of the church was initiated within the framework of the mission endeavour. The missionaries were among the first to look for ways and styles of witness in unity, recognizing that the scandal of Christian divisions and denominational rivalries hindered greatly the impact of their message.

2. The concern for mission and evangelism in unity has been constantly on the ecumenical agenda, especially since 1961 when the International Missionary Council merged with the World Council of Churches. In this context, the then Commission on World Mission and Evangelism issued in 1982 "Mission and Evangelism: An Ecumenical Affirmation". This statement summed up, in a comprehensive way, a number of the most important aspects and facets of mission, including diverse understandings of mission and its biblical and theological basis. Appropriating understandings already reached in the debates of the previous decade and enlarging them in a wider perspective, that document articulated ecumenical affirmations on mission and evangelism in the context of the world of the early 1980s.

3. The 1982 statement, which was approved by the WCC central committee, was received warmly and widely by the churches. It has been used by mission agencies, theological schools, local congregations and individual Christians. It has fermented, during these decades, new understandings of mission and evangelism and has inspired, provoked and strengthened the longing for witness in unity. It has reached far beyond the frontiers of the member churches of the WCC.

4. Since 1982 many of the world's realities have changed, confronting the churches with new mission challenges. Two world mission conferences have been held under WCC auspices, in San Antonio, USA (1989) and Salvador, Brazil (1996).

Important mission issues were raised also in the WCC seventh assembly in Canberra, Australia (1991). In the context of the new world situation and fresh missiological insights and learnings, a number of WCC member churches requested that a new statement on mission and evangelism be elaborated to assist the churches together to respond with an appropriate and meaningful mission praxis.

5. In response to such requests, the WCC decided to undertake the development of a further statement to assist Christians and the churches in their task of mission and evangelism in unity at the turn of the millennium. The present text, which has been adopted in March 2000 by the WCC's Commission on World Mission and Evangelism (CWME) as a study document, is offered in the hope that it will stimulate reflection on the nature, content and implications of the gospel of Jesus Christ in the varied but inter-related contexts of their life and faithful witness to the gospel, to the end that all people everywhere may have the opportunity to hear and to believe.

6. The present document does not replace the 1982 statement; neither does it promote a theology of mission different from what was agreed upon ecumenically in that statement. It has an identity of its own. *It attempts to articulate anew the churches' commitment to mission and evangelism in unity within the context of the challenges facing them today.*

7. **Use of terminology.** For some Christians and churches the terms "mission" and "evangelism", although related, are perceived and used differently; for others the two are virtually identical in both meaning and content. In the present document the two terms are used with some differentiation.

a) "Mission" carries a holistic understanding: the proclamation and sharing of the good news of the gospel by word (*kerygma*), deed (*diakonia*), prayer and worship (*leiturgia*) and the everyday witness of the Christian life (*martyria*); teaching as building up and strengthening people in their relationship with God and each other; and healing as whole-ness and reconciliation into koinonia - communion with God, communion with people, and communion with creation as a whole.

b) "Evangelism", while not excluding the different dimen-sions of mission, focuses on explicit and intentional voicing of the gospel, including the invitation to personal conversion to a new life in Christ and to discipleship.

8. The expression "mission in unity" refers to the search for ways of witnessing together in unity and cooperation - despite differing ecclesiologies - within the context of the burning chal-lenges facing churches everywhere today "so that the world may believe" (John 17:21), avoiding any form of confessional rival-ry or competition. This does not imply an unrealistic super-church ecclesiology; neither does it deny the intrinsic relation-ship between mission and ecclesiology.

A. Mission and Evangelism in Unity: An Imperative and Vocation

9. Mission is central to Christian faith and theology. It is not an option but is rather an existential calling and vocation. Mission is constitutive of and conditions the very being of the church and of all Christians.

10. The God revealed by the scriptures is not static but rather relational and missionary: a God who has always been manifest-ed as the Lord of history, leading God's people towards fullness of life through the covenants, the law, and the prophets who voiced God's will and interpreted the signs of the times; a God who came into the world through the incarnated Son, our Lord Jesus Christ, who, taking human flesh, shared our human condi-tion and became one of us, died on the cross and rose from the dead; a God who, in the power of the Holy Spirit, loves, cares for and sustains humanity and the whole of creation, leading them towards salvation and transfiguration.

11. The mission of God (*missio Dei*) has no limits or barriers; it has been addressed to and has been at work within the entire human race and the whole of creation throughout history. Jesus' parables of the good Samaritan and the sheep and the goats and his dialogue with the Syro-Phoenician woman clearly point in that direction. The early church apologists, in the framework of the dialogue with the people of their time, developed this idea further. On the basis of John 1, they explained that the Logos (Word), God's co-eternal and consubstantial Son, was and is present with the Father and the Holy Spirit in all God's acts, and that through the Word the world was created: God spoke, and "the Spirit swept over the face of the waters" (Gen. 1:2). In the Holy Spirit, they said, God spoke clearly and explicitly through the Word not only to the prophets of the Old Testament but also (though in a different way) to people of other nations and religions. When the fullness of time had come (Gal. 4:4), the very same Word "became flesh and lived among us" (John 1:14), coming to "his own" (John 1:11).

12. A trinitarian approach to the *missio Dei* is therefore important. On the one hand, this promotes a more inclusive understanding of God's presence and work in the whole world and among all people, implying that signs of God's presence can and should be identified, affirmed and worked with even in the most unexpected places. On the other hand, by clearly affirming that the Father and the Spirit are always and in all circumstances present and at work together with the Word, the temptation to separate the presence of God or the Spirit from the Son of God, Jesus Christ, will be avoided.

13. The mission of God (*missio Dei*) is the source of and basis for the mission of the church, the body of Christ. Through Christ in the Holy Spirit, God indwells the church, empowering and energizing its members. Thus mission becomes for Christians an urgent inner compulsion, even a powerful test and criterion for authentic life in Christ, rooted in the profound demands of Christ's love, to invite others to share in the fullness of life Jesus

came to bring (John 10:10). Participating in God's mission, should be natural for all Christians and all churches, not only for particular individuals or specialized groups. The Holy Spirit transforms Christians into living, courageous and bold witnesses (cf. Acts 1:8). "We cannot keep from speaking about what we have seen and heard" (Acts 4:20) was the response of Peter and John when they were ordered to keep silent about Jesus; or, in Paul's words, "If I proclaim the gospel, this gives me no ground for boasting, for an obligation is laid on me, and woe betide me if I do not proclaim the gospel!"(1 Cor. 9:16).

14. Christians are called through metanoia to "have the mind of Christ" (1 Cor. 2:16), to be agents of God's mission in the world (Matt. 28:19-20, Mark 16:15), to identify the signs of God's presence, affirming and promoting them by witnessing to and cooperating with all people of good will, and to be co workers with God (1 Cor. 4:1) for the transfiguration of the whole of creation. Thus, the goal of mission is "a reconciled humanity and renewed creation", and "the vision of God uniting all things in Christ is the driving force of its life and sharing".[1] "The church is sent into the world to call people and nations to repentance, to announce forgiveness of sin and a new beginning in relations with God and with neighbours through Jesus Christ."[2]

15. The mission of the church in the power of the Spirit is to call people into communion with God, with one another and with creation. In so doing, the church must honour the intrinsic and inseparable relationship between mission and unity. The church has the responsibility to live out the unity for which Jesus prayed for his people: "that they may all be one... so that the world may believe" (John 17:21). This conviction must be proclaimed and witnessed to in the community into which people are invited.

16. Mission in Christ's way is *holistic*, for the whole person and the totality of life are inseparable in God's plan of salvation accomplished in Jesus Christ. It is *local* - "the primary responsi-

bility for mission, where there is a local church, is with that church in its own place". It is also *universal*, that is, to all peoples, beyond all frontiers of race, caste, gender, culture, nation - to "the ends of the earth" in every sense (cf. Acts 1:8; Mark 16:15; Luke 24:47).[3]

17. "To tell the story [of Jesus Christ] is the specific privilege of the churches within God's overall mission."[4] Evangelism includes explication of the gospel - "accounting for the hope that is in you" (1 Pet. 3:15) - as well as an invitation to believe in the triune God, become a disciple of Christ and join the community of an existing local church. "Proclamation of Jesus Christ requires a personal response. The living Word of God is never external, unrelational, disconnected, but always calling for personal conversion and relational communion. Such a conversion is more than appropriation of a message: it is a commitment to Jesus Christ, imitating his death and resurrection in a very visible and tangible way. That which begins with a personal commitment must, however, immediately lead into a relationship with other members of the body of Christ, the local witnessing community."[5]

B. Context of Mission Today: Contemporary Trends

18. A major facet of the contemporary context of mission is that of **globalization** - a relatively recent phenomenon having to do with economic developments, changes in means of global communication and the consequent imposition of a new monoculture and a related set of values on most societies. These trends are of course not totally new; but the political changes at the end of the 1980s allow them now to influence the whole world unhindered by any global counter force.

19. A crucial aspect of globalization is the increasing liberalization of the economy, characterized by the unlimited flow of capital all over the world in search of maximum profit in the short term. These financial operations have rules of their own, mostly without reference to real production of economic

goods or services. They have unpredictable effects and damage national economies, leaving governments and international institutions with virtually no possibility of influencing them. In that sense, globalization challenges and is a threat to the very basis of human society.

20. In the wake of the collapse of communism, the free market has become the sole overall functioning system. Economics have become the major criteria for human relationships. The whole realm of present day social realities, including human beings themselves, is defined and referred to in economic and financial categories. In the global market, people matter insofar as they are consumers. Only those who are stronger and more competitive survive. Those who have no value for the market - people who are poor, sick, unemployed, powerless - are simply pushed to the fringes of society. Exclusion, accompanied by structural, spiritual and physical violence, has reached intolerable levels in most parts of the world. The impact of globalization on the so-called developing countries and regions is a life-and-death issue: provision for fundamental human needs such as shelter, health care, nutrition and education among the poorest is actually less than it was thirty years ago. This has resulted in the increasing "economic migration" of workers, rural and indigenous people, looking for jobs or expelled from their lands.

21. Among the consequences of this trend is the increasing degradation of the environment. Nature in many places is savagely exploited, resulting in ecological crises and disasters which threaten even the continuation of life on our planet.

22. A second aspect of globalization has to do with new information technology and mass communication possibilities, the accelerated development and growth of which is transforming human and social relations. At a first glance, it seems that the ancient dream of making the world one is finally becoming a reality. The globe seems to be becoming very small. People in all parts of the world can and do benefit from new technological

developments. Intercommunication is flourishing. Recent scientific and medical discoveries can be shared globally and instantaneously. The new electronic communication tools can be used for human progress, for creating a more transparent and open world, for disseminating information on abuses of human rights and the crimes of dictators. They help peoples' movements and churches throughout the world to network more efficiently. But they are also used by racist and criminal groups and, especially, by those who within seconds move millions of dollars to wherever they will be able to take the largest profit. And those who do not have access to the new communication networks suffer from new exclusion.

23. Through processes of globalization, the values of **post-modernity**, rooted in Western cultures, are spreading rapidly across the globe. The very identities of people are in danger of being diluted or weakened in the melting pot of the powerfully tempting and attractive monoculture and its new set of values. The very notion of nationhood itself is severely challenged. Individualism is preferred to life in community. Traditional values which formerly were lived as public values are today being privatized. Even religion is treated as merely a private matter. Personal experience takes the place of reason, knowledge and understanding. Images are preferred to words and have a greater impact on people in terms of advertising, promoting or conveying "truths" and goods. The importance of the present moment is emphasized; the past and future do not really matter. People are persuaded to believe that they are masters of their own lives and are therefore free to pick and choose what suits themselves.

24. The expanding monoculture does not yet affect the whole world to the same degree. The people most influenced by the new cultural trends are the ones who can participate in the market, especially those in the power centres of each country and region. How the values of post-modernity will interact with the various human cultures is not entirely predictable. Resistance has grown against this subtle new form of imperialism, from

grassroots organizations and communities, Indigenous peoples, churches of the poor and cultures rooted in strong religious world-views.

25. The centripetal forces of globalization are accompanied by centrifugal forces of fragmentation, which are being felt ever more acutely. This **fragmentation** is being experienced at personal, national and international levels. Traditional family patterns are breaking down. Divorces have reached an unprecedented rate and the number of one parent families is growing in many places. At the national level, in the vacuum created by the collapse of the totalitarian regimes in Eastern Europe and the ramifications of that collapse in the rest of the world, turmoil, tensions and fragmentation have arisen among and within the somewhat artificial statal units inherited from the pre 1989 period. New states have emerged along ethnic and tribal lines. Peoples who have lived together for generations can no longer stand one another. Cultural and ethnic identities are being used to oppress other identities. "Ethnic cleansing" and genocides are taking place in many parts of the world, bringing immense suffering, increasing hatred and setting the stage for further violence towards humankind and creation.

26. The contemporary context of mission includes **trends within the churches** as well. In many parts of the world, churches are growing dramatically. This is true of churches - including so-called mainline churches - in disadvantaged communities, Pentecostal or African instituted churches and charismatic renewal movements, especially but not exclusively in the South. Even in the wealthier countries, where post modernity is influencing attitudes and beliefs, new ways of "being church" in terms of community life and worship are experienced. And a growing number of strong missionary movements reaching out to other parts of the world are based in the South.

27. Some but not all of these churches appear to be striving for holistic witness to the gospel. Indeed, the highly competitive

environment of the free market is reinforcing many churches and para church movements in their perception of mission as the effort to attract and recruit new "customers", while retaining the old ones. Their programmes and doctrines are presented as "religious products", which must be appealing and attractive to potential new members. They evaluate the success of their mission in terms of growth, of numbers of converts or of newly planted churches. Unfortunately, very often their "new members" already belonged to other churches. Thus proselytism (as competition and "sheep-stealing") is one of the sharp contemporary issues facing the churches.

28. After so many decades of ecumenical dialogue and life together, there is a paradoxical resurgence of confessionalism today, undoubtedly linked to the fragmentation process. Denominations are signs of the richness of charisms and spiritual gifts within the household of God when they positively contribute to a better common understanding of the gospel and the mission of the church in the process towards unity. But many churches seem to be more concerned about affirming and strengthening their own confessional and denominational identities than about ecumenical endeavours. Some prefer to do their missionary and diaconal work alone, in parallel or even in competition with others, and the number of fundamentalist and anti ecumenical Christian groups seems to be on the increase.

29. Finally, new religious movements of various kinds are proliferating everywhere, recruiting their adherents from traditionally Christian families, even from among active church members. The churches and their teachings are often attacked and denounced while new, modern, more attractive messages are promoted.

30. The above brief description of the overall context does not, of course, take into consideration the important variations and even opposite emphases in different regions and local situations. Nevertheless, this is the "world" in which the churches are

called to give clear, authentic witness to the gospel and to develop viable alternatives for the future which are faithful to mission in Christ's way.[6]

C. Mission Paradigms for our Times

1. Called to participate in God's mission for fullness of life

31. The rapidly spreading processes of globalization, expressed in the savage and uncontrolled free-market economy and in high technology which reduces the value of the whole of reality to economic and financial categories, confronts the mission of the church with the growing phenomenon of dehumanization. In contexts of poverty and inhuman exploitation this is experienced as a daily struggle for the most elementary basics of life, even for life itself. In other contexts, within a framework of hopelessness, discouragement and estrangement - experienced as lack of meaning in the present and lack of hope for the future - the suicide rate (especially among young people) is growing and apathy is becoming fashionable. In all cases, the church is called to proclaim the good news of Jesus Christ with boldness and to participate in God's mission for fullness of life. It is the mission of the church to reaffirm with courage and persistence the unique and eternal value of each human person as being created in the image of the holy, mighty and immortal God.

32. Within a context of human reductionism and spiritual captivity, there are signs of the search for meaning, fulfilment and spirituality. A fresh new missionary enthusiasm is evident today and new Christian communities are being established.

33. On the other hand, the growth of new religious movements and the search of youth in particular for religious experiences is becoming a characteristic of our time. Often, however, such searches and consequent experiences have brought painful results, as the dominating spirit of today's context has put its mark even on attempts towards a liberating, fulfilling spirituality. Seen through the contemporary lens of individual fulfilment

and experience, spirituality is often understood as a set of techniques and methods for personal growth, holistic health, clarity of mind, control of senses. In other words, the source of fulfilment and meaning is seen not in a relationship with a personal God who is both transcendent and immanent, but rather in the attempt to "awaken" the godly powers which are already present, though dormant, in human beings.

34. In the face of such challenges, it is the mission of the church to encounter people's needs and searches, helping them to discover adequate answers and directions on the basis of the scriptures and the experience of the church throughout the ages. It is timely to witness in word and deed that the source of life, meaning and fulfilment is the triune God fully revealed and manifested in the life of Jesus of Nazareth. By his death on the cross, death was defeated; and through his resurrection, authentic meaning and the final goal and vocation of humanity was transformed into life in its fullness. In the Christian life, therefore, taking up one's own cross - with all the pains that the death of the old self may imply - leads always to a joyful and fulfilling experience of resurrection into a new creation (2 Cor. 5:17). From the experiences of "so great a cloud of witnesses" (Heb. 12:1) over the centuries, it is therefore imperative to convey the message that Christian spirituality leads to holistic healing, community and fullness of life in relationship with God, other people and the whole of creation.

35. Religion as life in Christ and consciousness of a rediscovered full and authentic human identity, therefore, cannot be simply a private matter. Rather it shapes one's whole perspective, vision and ways of relating to others. Christians cannot lead dichotomic lives: religious life and secular life are a single reality. Life itself should be a continuous liturgy of loving relationships with God, the source of life, and with other people and the whole of creation. Thus all realities faced by human beings in their daily lives may be subjects of theological reflection. Faith touches all realms of life - including social and economic jus-

tice, politics, ethics, biogenetics and the environment - and enables appropriate and prophetic answers and directions from that specific perspective.

36. The church is also called to offer, out of its experience over the centuries, concrete alternative paradigms to the consumerist ideology of globalization. To the temptation of dominion it must set limits and use its power to say "no more"; to the temptation of possession and ownership, the ascesis of the early Christians who refrained from eating and shared their food and belongings with the needy and dispossessed; to the temptation of power, the prophetic voice; to the temptation of proclaiming a truncated and partial message tailored to the preferences and expectations of people of our time, the accurate and whole message of the gospel - "the whole church [challenged] to take the whole gospel to the whole world".[7]

2. *Called to life in community*

37. Another great challenge facing Christian mission in our time, especially in the North, is individualism, which penetrates and influences all spheres of life. The individual seems to be considered the sole norm of reality and existence. Society and community are losing their traditional, historical meaning and value. This trend in human relationships also affects the traditional understanding of the relationship between Christians and the church in the process of salvation. Many perceive salvation as a matter between an individual and God, and do not see the role of the community of faith, the church. They may affirm faith in God, but may severely challenge or even deny the significance of the church as an instrument for relationship to God, other people and the whole of creation, as well as the concept of salvation in and through community.

38. In the face of such a trend, which is affecting the very fabric of human society in general and of Christian community in particular, the church is called to proclaim God's will and intention for the world. Created in the image of the triune God - who is by

definition an eternal communion of life and love - human beings are by nature relational. The relational dimension of human life is a given, ontological reality. Any authentic anthropology, therefore, must be relational and communitarian.

39. The Trinity, the source and image of our existence, shows the importance of diversity, otherness and intrinsic relationships in constituting a community. The members of a community are different, with different gifts, functions, strengths and weaknesses (if the members were all the same, the body could not be constituted [1 Cor. 12]). The community therefore requires diversity and otherness. These however should be neither over against nor parallel to but complementary to one another.

40. The Salvador conference highlighted the importance that the gospel places on the different identities that constitute community. Such identities, be they national, cultural, historical or religious, are affirmed by the gospel so long as they lead in the direction of relationship and communion. Identities which attempt to further their own interests at the expense of others - demonstrated, for example, in xenophobia, "ethnic cleansing", racism, religious intolerance and fanaticism - thus disrupting and destroying the koinonia, are denied and refuted by the same gospel.

41. An authentic Christian community should be both local and catholic (from *kata holon,* meaning "according to the whole"). Catholicity, which is a mark of the authenticity of any Christian community, is in fact based on the diversity of local identities in complementary communion with one another.

42. Such theological affirmations have important implications for the mission praxis of the church. The Salvador conference, for example, touched on the issue of indigenous spirituality within the framework of the relationship between the gospel and cultures. If the church is a koinonia of convergent and complementary diversities, it is necessary to seek ways in which expressions of Christian theology, liturgy and spirituality in

forms other than the traditional and historical ones can be integrated and incorporated in the manifold spectrum.

43. In the same perspective arises the issue of the inclusive community of women and men as equal and complementary partners in the life of the church. The recognition of the role of women in the mission of the church, bringing fullness and integrity to human and church community, is a sine qua non. To that end, attention should be drawn to the manifold examples in church history of preaching, witnessing and martyred women and to the women saints who, because of their faithfulness in proclaiming the gospel, are venerated as "equal to the apostles".

44. On the basis of the recognition that mission should begin with listening and learning rather than preaching, teaching and proclaiming, a new approach may be called for in relation to the growth of "implicit religion" in many societies. Many people strongly confess faith in God but have little or no relationship with the church. Some practise at home their own form of "liturgy" and devotion. Such practices have often been regarded by the church as mere traditions, folklore or even superstition. Perhaps they could rather be considered as a sincere search for the living God, for fullness of life and meaning - however different they may be from the worship of a local congregation - and become a basis on which to build and to witness with love to the message of the gospel.

3. Called to incarnate the gospel within each culture

45. "Culture shapes the human voice that answers the voice of Christ," said the Bangkok world mission conference in 1973. Recent developments have again placed the inseparable relation between the gospel and human cultures on the mission agenda. At the Canberra assembly (1991) and in other circles there have been heated debates about inculturation theologies and attempts to articulate the gospel in terms very different from the traditions of some of the historical churches. Experiences shared during the Ecumenical Decade of Churches in Solidarity with

Women demonstrated how cultures have sometimes been mis-used for power purposes and become oppressive. During the 1990s the world has witnessed an increasing affirmation of local identities, often leading to violent conflicts and persecution on ethnic and cultural grounds, sometimes with direct or indirect support by Christians or churches. Such a context makes it urgent for mission reflection to take up afresh the challenge of inculturation.

46. The Salvador conference strongly affirmed that "there is no way of being human without participating in culture, for it is through culture that identity is created".[8] Culture is interpreted both as a result of God's grace and as an expression of human creativity. In any actual context, it must be stressed that culture is intrinsically neither good nor bad, but has the potential for both - and is thus ambiguous.

47. In recent ecumenical discussions, culture has been under-stood in a very broad sense as including all aspects of human effort. "Each community has a culture - by which is meant the totality of what constitutes its life, all that is essential for rela-tionships among its members, and its relationships with God and with the natural environment."[9] This means that religion is part of culture, often even at its heart. One cannot speak of cultures without including people's religious beliefs and value systems.

48. God's mission has been revealed as incarnational. Mission in Christ's way thus cannot but be rooted in a certain context, con-cretely addressing the challenges in that specific context. Hence the gospel is and must be "translatable". In each and every situ-ation, the churches' witness to Christ must be rooted in the local culture so that authentically inculturated faith communities may develop. Clearly, all cultures can express the love of God and no culture has the right to consider itself the exclusive norm for God's relationship with human beings.

49. When the gospel interacts authentically with a culture, it becomes rooted in that culture and opens up biblical and theo-

logical meaning for its time and place. The gospel will affirm some aspects of a culture, while challenging, critiquing and transforming others. Through such processes, cultures may be transfigured and become bearers of the gospel. At the same time, cultures nourish, illuminate, enrich and challenge the understanding and articulation of the gospel.

50. The gospel challenges aspects of cultures which produce or perpetuate injustice, suppress human rights or hinder a sustainable relationship towards creation. There is now need to go beyond certain inculturation theologies. Cultural and ethnic identity is a gift of God, but it must not be used to reject and oppress other identities. Identity should be defined not in opposition to, in competition with or in fear of others, but rather as complementary. "The gospel reconciles and unites people of all identities into a new community in which the primary and ultimate identity is identity in Jesus Christ (Gal. 3:28)."[10]

51. The debate over the inter relation between the gospel and cultures has specific significance for Indigenous peoples, who suffered greatly from missionary endeavours and colonial conquest, in the course of which their cultures and religions were described mostly as "pagan", in need of the gospel and "civilization". Later the terminology changed, but Indigenous peoples were still considered mainly as "objects" of the churches' witness, as "poor" in need of economic or development aid. In more recent theologies, which affirmed "God's preferential option for the poor", marginalized people were indeed considered as bearers - that is, subjects - of a new mission movement from the so-called periphery to the centre. But these theologies still functioned on the basis of socio-economic categories, neglecting people's religious heritage. Now, Indigenous peoples are challenging the churches to recognize the richness of their culture and spirituality, which emphasizes interconnectedness and reciprocity with the whole creation. They are asking the churches to work in real partnership with them, doing mission together as equals, in mutual sharing.

52. In any culture the message of Christ must be proclaimed in language and symbols adapted to that culture and in ways that are relevant to people's life experiences. There are different approaches to culturally sensitive evangelism. For some people and churches, such witness is implicit when churches regularly celebrate the liturgy, including in it, where appropriate, local cultural symbols. Others suggest that "a way of making non intrusive contact with communities of other cultures is that of 'presence'. An effort is first made to get to know and understand people in that community, and sincerely to listen to and learn from them... At the right time people could be invited to participate in the story of the gospel."[11] In some cases the gospel may best be conveyed by silent solidarity or be revealed through a deeply spiritual way of life. In contexts which are hostile to the voicing of the gospel, witness could take place through providing "a 'safe space' for spirituality to germinate, where the Jesus story can be revealed".[12] Others insist that in most contexts explicit testimony is called for - that there is no substitute for preaching the word, following the manifold impulses and dynamics of the Holy Spirit.

53. Attention should always be given to a holistic and balanced approach to the praxis of mission; the temptation to emphasize one aspect and ignore others should be avoided. Authentic evangelism must always include both witness and unconditional loving service. As San Antonio affirmed: "The 'material gospel' and the 'spiritual gospel' have to be one, as was true of the ministry of Jesus... There is no evangelism without solidarity; there is no Christian solidarity that does not involve sharing the message of God's coming reign."[13]

54. Dynamic interactions between the gospel and cultures inevitably raise the question of syncretism, for each inculturation of the gospel touches beliefs, rites, religious community structures. Among churches the term "syncretism" is understood in different ways. For some, the integrity of the gospel message is diminished when it is fused with certain elements of the con-

text in which it is being inculturated; they understand syncretism as betrayal of the gospel. For others, there can be no creative building up of communities and theologies in any culture without syncretism. The question then is whether a specific inculturation helps or hinders faithful witness to the gospel in its fullness.

55. Differences in interpretation have to do with the understanding of the term "gospel" and of the work of the Holy Spirit in various cultures. These questions must be handled carefully, since accusations of syncretism often reflect and reinforce power imbalances between churches. The Salvador conference pointed to the need for a framework for intercultural hermeneutics (theory of interpretation of the gospel). It further indicated the need for criteria for assessing in dialogue with other churches the appropriateness of particular contextual expressions of the gospel. Such criteria include: "faithfulness to God's self disclosure in the totality of the scriptures; commitment to a life-style and action in harmony with the reign of God; openness to the wisdom of the communion of saints across space and time; [and] relevance to the context".[14]

4. Called to witness and dialogue

56. The phenomenon of religious pluralism has become one of the most serious overall challenges to Christian mission for the coming century. Witness in multifaith societies has traditionally been considered a concern primarily of churches and missionaries in Africa, Asia, the Middle East and other parts of the world. In recent years, however, through increased migration, religious pluralism has become a global reality. In some places Christians enjoy freedom and live and cooperate with others in a spirit of mutual respect and understanding. In other places, however, there is growing religious intolerance.

57. In Europe and North America (traditionally Christian territories), the growing presence in local communities of people of other faiths poses serious challenges for the mission activities of the churches. Christians in historically multifaith societies have

over the centuries gained experience of how to live and witness in such contexts. New challenges are arising even for them, however, in terms of how the Christian commitment to mission and evangelism may be affirmed with faithfulness to the gospel as well as love and respect for the other.

58. Such challenges inevitably raise theological questions concerning the nature of witness among people of other religious convictions, in relation to the nature of salvation itself. There is little consensus on this in the broader ecumenical movement. In the San Antonio and Salvador mission conferences, the situation was summarized through the following affirmations: "We cannot point to any other way of salvation than Jesus Christ; at the same time we cannot set limits to the saving power of God."[15] There is a tension between these two statements, a tension which has not yet been resolved.

59. Among people engaged in mission, there is a growing (though not unchallenged) recognition that God is at work outside the churches - though exactly *how* God is at work in any religious community is impossible to define. But people in mission do indeed discover "glimpses" of God's presence and activity among people of other religious traditions. Contemporary experience meets ancient tradition: early Christian theologians such as Justin Martyr spoke of "the seeds of the word" among the cultures of the world; others, such as Eusebius of Caesarea, used the term "evangelical preparation", also referred to in Paul VI's encyclical on evangelism as well as in the Salvador texts.

60. Thus an open question requiring further reflection and sharing among Christians engaged in mission relates to the discernment of the signs of the Spirit's presence among people of other faiths or no faith. The Salvador conference hinted at such signs when pointing to expressions of love, values such as humility, openness to God and to others, as well as commitments to justice, solidarity and non-violent means of resolving conflict. Galatians 5:22 23, which speaks of the fruit of the Spirit, was cited as a helpful guide for this discernment.

61. In mission there is place both for the proclamation of the good news of Jesus Christ and for dialogue with people of other faiths. According to the situation and the charisms of Christians in that situation, the emphasis may differ. Many would claim, however, that the only proper mode of living in community is dialogical. Reaffirming the evangelistic mandate of Christians, the San Antonio conference pointed out that "our ministry of witness among people of other faiths presupposes our *presence* with them, *sensitivity* to their deepest faith commitments and experiences, *willingness* to be their servants for Christ's sake, *affirmation* of what God has done and is doing among them, and *love* for them... We are called to be *witnesses* to others, not judges of them."[16] If mission is to be in Christ's way, there cannot be evangelism without openness to others and readiness to discover his presence also where it is not expected.

62. On the other hand, there is no real dialogue if the religious identity and beliefs of the partners are not made clear. In that sense, it can be affirmed that witness precedes dialogue. To speak of evangelism means to emphasize the proclamation of God's offer of freedom and reconciliation, together with the invitation to join those who follow Christ and work for the reign of God. Dialogue is a form of witness to Jesus' commandment to love one's neighbour - even one's enemy - and may be, in certain contexts, the only way to be faithful to a humble, kenotic style of mission, following Christ's vulnerable life in service, not domination.

5. Called to proclaim the truth of the gospel

63. One of the great challenges of our times - and one which touches the very heart of the Christian message - is the growing phenomenon of relativism, as developed especially among Western philosophers and scientists. In post modern thinking, the notion of absolute and universal truth, whether in the political, social, economic or even religious realm, is drastically questioned or rejected. Truth is rather seen as a matter of individual

discernment through a personal "pick-and-choose" preference, experience and decision. Rather than objective, universal and absolute "truth", there are "truths" parallel to and cohabiting with one another.

64. Such an understanding of and approach to truth not only influences much of day-to-day life in particular the industrialized countries, but also has a deep impact on the churches' witness and on participation in the ecumenical movement.

65. This approach challenges traditional patterns of Christian mission. People defending such a world-view plead for a new missionary understanding, style and praxis more appropriate to contemporary realities. They ask to give up the "arrogant" attitude of conveying Christianity as the only truth leading to salvation and request that it be presented rather more humbly and decently as one of many truths found in various religions or in creation in general. They argue that in theory these other truths have a similar value and final goal, with only peronal choices making a qualitative difference between them.

66. In the ecumenical field, notions such as "unity", "consensus" and "apostolic truth" are questioned and, for some, have even acquired a pejorative connotation. A more recent ecumenical vision includes the search for a new paradigm and image which could accommodate a diversity of truths under the same roof without diluting or annihilating any in the process of trying to bring them into convergence, for the sake of reaching one common and binding apostolic truth.

67. Glimpses of directions and partial responses to the challenges raised by relativism have been proffered; sharper and more coherent responses are still needed. What is the relationship between the truth of the gospel that Christians are called to proclaim concerning the uniqueness of Jesus Christ, "the way, and the truth, and the life" (John 14:6), and the truth of "the gospel before the gospel", and what are the consequences for the unity of the church?

6. *Called to witness in unity*

68. In recent decades the churches have become ever more aware of the necessity to engage in mission together, in cooperation and mutual accountability: hence mission partnerships have been established, some international mission structures transformed, and common projects undertaken. The same period, however, has seen an escalation of confessional rivalries and competition in mission in many parts of the world. These realities compel the ecumenical family to re-examine issues of mission in unity, cooperation among the churches, common witness and proselytism, and to work towards more responsible relationships in mission.

69. Common witness is "the witness that the churches, even while separated, bear together, especially through joint efforts, by manifesting whatever divine gifts of truth and life they already share and experience in common".[17] Authentic common witness presupposes respect for and understanding of other traditions and confessions. What should be emphasized is that which is common and can be done together, rather than the barriers which separate. There is more that unites the churches than separates them. These unifying elements should be looked for in building up witness in unity.

70. Mission and religious liberty, including the freedom to change one's religion or belief, are intrinsically related. Mission cannot be imposed by any means on anyone. On the other hand, one's own freedom must always respect, affirm and promote the freedom of others; it must not contravene the golden rule: "In everything do to others as you would have them do to you" (Matt. 7:12).

71. Proselytism, a positive term in early Christian times used to designate a person of another faith converting to Christianity, took in later centuries a negative connotation due to changes in content, motivation, spirit and methods of "evangelism". It is now generally used to mean "the encouragement of Christians

who belong to a church to change their denominational allegiance, through ways and means that contradict the spirit of Christian love, violate the freedom of the human person and diminish trust in the Christian witness of the church".[18] Proselytism is "the corruption of witness".[19]

72. Common witness is constructive: it enriches, challenges, strengthens and builds up solid Christian relationships and fellowship. Proselytism is a perversion of authentic Christian witness and thus a counter-witness. It does not build up but destroys. It brings about tensions, scandal and division, and is thus a destabilizing factor for the witness of the church in the world. It is always a wounding of koinonia, creating not koinonia but antagonistic parties.

73. As new contexts call for new initiatives in proclaiming the gospel in the face of common challenges, the churches are called to identify ways of witnessing in unity, of partnership and cooperation and of responsible relationships in mission. In order to reach such a mutually enriching missionary ethos, the churches must:

a) repent of past failures and reflect more self-critically on their ways of relating to one another and their methods of evangelizing;

b) renounce all forms of denominational competition and rivalry and the temptation to proselytize members of other Christian traditions;

c) avoid establishing parallel ecclesial structures, but rather stimulate, help and cooperate with the existing local churches in their evangelistic work;

d) condemn any manipulation of humanitarian assistance to individual Christians or churches to induce people into changing their denominational allegiance or to further the missionary goals of one church at the expense of another;

e) help people who are in process of changing their church allegiance to discern whether they are being guided by worthy or unworthy motives (such as social advancement or better life opportunities);

f) learn to "speak the truth in love" to one another when they consider others to be proselytizing or engaging in dishonest practices in evangelism.

74. This Christian fellowship and partnership will not be possible unless Christians and churches:

a) listen to one another in genuine dialogue aimed at overcoming ignorance, prejudices or misunderstandings, understanding their differences in the perspective of Christian unity and avoiding unjust accusations, polemics, disagreements and rejection;

b) ensure greater sharing of information and accountability in mission at all levels, including prior consultation with the church in an area to see what are the possibilities of missionary collaboration and witness in unity;

c) demonstrate willingness to learn from others - for example, from their dynamism, enthusiasm and joy in mission, their sense of community, their rejoicing in the Spirit, their spirituality;

d) make greater efforts for inner renewal in their own traditions and cultural contexts;

e) make greater efforts to educate their own faithful in local congregations, Sunday schools, training centres and seminaries to respect and love members of other churches as sisters and brothers in Christ.

75. Ecumenical convictions on mission in unity may lead to the formulation of a **covenant** concerning relationships in mission. Among the basic convictions and commitments in mission which could be included are the following:

76. Convictions

a) Mission begins in the heart of the triune God. The love which binds together the persons of the Holy Trinity overflows in a great outpouring of love for humankind and all creation.

b) God calls the church in Jesus Christ and empowers it by the Holy Spirit to be a partner in God's mission, bearing witness to the gospel of the love of God made clear in the life, death and resurrection of Jesus Christ, and inviting people to become disciples of Christ.

c) Christian mission involves a holistic response through evangelistic and diaconal work to reach out to people in their experience of exclusion, brokenness and meaninglessness. It involves the empowerment, affirmation and renewal of people in their hope for fullness of life.

d) All baptized Christians are commissioned to bear witness to the gospel of Christ and all are accountable to the body of Christ for their witness; all need to find a home in a local worshipping community through which to exercise their accountability to the body.

77. Commitments

a) Impelled by the love of Christ, we commit ourselves to work to ensure that all our neighbours in every place, near and far, have the opportunity to hear and respond to the gospel of Jesus Christ.

b) We acknowledge that the primary responsibility for mission in any place rests with the church in that place.

c) Where missionaries or funds are sent by our church to a place where there is already a Christian church, that will be done in a negotiated, mutually acceptable, respectful arrangement, with equal participation of all parties in the decision-making process.

d) We acknowledge that in our partnerships all partners have gifts to offer and all have need to learn, receive and be enriched by the relationship; so the relationship must allow for the reciprocal sharing of both needs and gifts.

e) We acknowledge that all the churches' resources belong to God, and that the wealth of the rich has often been derived from the exploitation of others.

f) We commit ourselves to make the relationship on all sides as transparent as possible concerning finance, theology, personnel, struggles, dilemmas, fears, hopes, ideas, stories - an open sharing that builds trust.

g) We recognize that nearly every intercultural encounter between churches is marked with an unequal distribution of power. Money, material possessions, state connections, history and other factors affect the way churches relate to each other. In entering into relationships in mission, we commit ourselves to guard against misuse of power and to strive for just relationships.

h) We recognize that it is important not to create dependency. Partnerships must lead to interdependence. We will seek through our partnerships to enable the emergence of authentic local cultural responses to the gospel in terms of liturgies, hymns, rituals, structures, institutions, theological formulations.

i) We believe that mission and unity are inseparably related. We therefore commit ourselves to encourage collaboration and structural unity between our mission agencies and our own church, between mission agencies, and between mission agencies and our partner churches. Where several churches already exist in a given area we commit ourselves to deliberately fostering a council of churches.

j) We recognize that mission and evangelism have been carried on almost entirely along denominational lines. We commit ourselves to undertake mission ecumenically, both locally and abroad, wherever possible.

k) In developing international partnerships in mission, we commit ourselves to giving priority to building solidarity with excluded and suffering people and communities in their struggles for fullness of life.

1. Cf. *Signs of the Spirit: Official Report of the Seventh Assembly*, Michael Kinnamon ed., WCC, 1991, p.100.

2 *Mission and Evangelism: An Ecumenical Affirmation*, WCC, 1982, see p.4 of this volume.

3 *Towards Common Witness: A Call to Adopt Responsible Relationships in Mission and to Renounce Proselytism*, WCC, 1997, see p.46 of this volume.

4 *Called to One Hope: The Gospel in Diverse Cultures,* official report of the conference on world mission and evangelism, Salvador, Brazil, 1996, Christopher Duraisingh ed., WCC, 1998, p.62.

5 *Proclaiming Christ Today,* report of an Orthodox-Evangelical consultation, Alexandria, Egypt, 1995, Huibert van Beek and Georges Lemopoulos eds, WCC, 1995, p.13.

6 Several commissioners expressed uneasiness because of the excessively negative description of globalization in this part of the document.

7 "The Lausanne Covenant", 1974, para. 6.

8 Salvador report, p.31.

9 *The San Antonio Report*, official report of the conference on world mission and evangelism, San Antonio, USA, 1989, Frederick R. Wilson ed., WCC, 1990, p.43.

10 Salvador report, p.46.

11 *Ibid.*, p.38.

12 *Ibid.*

13 San Antonio report, p.32.

14 Salvador report, p.67

15 Salvador report, p.62, quoting San Antonio report, p.32.

16 San Antonio report, p.26.

17 Thomas Stransky, "Common Witness", in *Dictionary of the Ecumenical Movement*, WCC, 1991, p.197; quoted in *Towards Common Witness*, see p.47 of this volume.

18 Report of the Orthodox consultation on "Mission and Proselytism", Sergiev Possad, Russia, 1995; quoted in *Towards Common Witness*, see p. 49 of this volume.

19 "Revised Report on 'Christian Witness, Proselytism and Religious Liberty in the Setting of the World Council of Churches'", *in Minutes and Reports of the Central Committee of the World Council of Churches, St Andrews, Scotland, August 1960*, WCC, 1960, p.214; quoted in *Towards Common Witness*, see p.49 of this volume. Statements and documents on common witness elaborated within the WCC framework include: "Christian Witness, Proselytism and Religious Liberty in the Setting of the WCC"(New Delhi, 1961), "Common Witness and Proselytism"(1970), "Common Witness"(1982), "The Challenge of Proselytism and the Calling to Common Witness"(1995), and "Towards Common Witness: A Call to Adopt Responsible Relationships in Mission and to Renounce Proselytism"(1997).

Mission as Ministry of Reconciliation

Presentation

This document offers reflections on mission as ministry of reconciliation from an ecumenical point of view and is shared by the Commission on World Mission and Evangelism (CWME) of the World Council of Churches as a document for reflection and study in preparation for the world mission conference in Athens in May 2005.[1] A first version of the document was drawn up in January 2004 by a group of ten missiologists and submitted to the CWME conference planning committee which adopted it as a study document.[2] That first version was submitted in October 2004 to the CWME Commission, together with important suggestions and reactions received from individual missiologists and theological institutions. The Commission decided to receive the paper and asked a small editorial group of commissioners and members of the first drafting group to revise and slightly expand it on certain points, taking into account the most significant reactions received as well as the discussions held at the Commission meeting itself. The present revised version was elaborated in January 2005 on the basis of those guidelines.

This is the first WCC collective document elaborating in some detail how a focus on the ministry of reconciliation, a vocation of the church described by St Paul in 2 Corinthians 5:18, shapes the content and method of mission, and what scope and significance it gives to mission. As such, this paper may be read as an outcome of a process of reflection started after the San Antonio world mission conference (1989) and reinforced by insights gained through the pneumatological focus given to mission at the WCC Canberra assembly in 1991.[3] Since then, reconciliation has grown in importance both in ecumenical social and political ethics as well as in missiology. Following the 1998 Harare assembly and the decision to launch the Decade to Overcome Violence - Churches Seeking Reconciliation and Peace, the "ministry of reconciliation" became one of the major foci of the programmatic work of the WCC. In 2001, the Commission on World Mission and Evangelism decided that reconciliation and healing would feature as central themes for the 2005 world mission conference.

The paper grounds its understanding of the ministry of reconciliation on a clear biblical-theological basis, followed by a summary of experiences made in various parts of the world. The document highlights a number of key issues to be taken into consideration for reconciliation to have some chance of being authentic in conflict and post-conflict situations. It draws consequences for an understanding of the mission of the church as a mediator and bridge-builder, a role which, however, must not be at the expense of witnessing to God's preferential option for the victims. The paper underlines the difficulty for the church to keep a balance between efforts at maintaining the communication between conflicting parties (its "in-betweenness") and a clear manifestation of its solidarity with the victims. The last chapters describe reconciliation as spirituality and as inspiration for a pastoral ministry and for ecumenical formation.

Together with the document on the healing mission of the church, also published in this book, this document provides a summary of the state of discussion on mission as ministry of reconciliation and healing in the WCC. It is offered as a resource for reflection and study on the significance and importance of mission at the beginning of the 21st century.

JM

1 It was first published on the website of the 2005 world mission conference as conference preparatory paper no. 10.
2 Published on the same website as conference preparatory paper no. 4. The conference planning committee was a sub-group of the Commission, composed of a dozen commissioners.
3 Both Christopher Duraisingh, at that time director of CWME and Philip Potter, WCC general secretary, emphasized the importance of reconciliation in papers they wrote interpreting the results of the San Antonio conference and/or preparing for the Canberra assembly. Cf. Jacques Matthey, "Editorial", and Klaus Schäfer, "Come, Holy Spirit, Heal and Reconcile", in IRM, vol. 94, no. 372, Jan. 2005.

Mission as Ministry of Reconciliation

1. Mission and reconciliation - an emerging paradigm

1. Mission is understood in different ways in various times and places, also among actors in the ecumenical movement. From time to time, there is an attempt at a more holistic interpretation of Christian witness. In 1982, the World Council of Churches (WCC) reached such a balanced understanding of mission, in its Ecumenical Affirmation on Mission and Evangelism.[1] Responding to the challenge of the gospel and the request of the time, that declaration combined the focus on sharing the gospel with the concern for the liberation of the poor. It remains until now the basic WCC text on mission and evangelism. Since the late 1980s new aspects emerged and mission has been increasingly connected with reconciliation and healing. The language of reconciliation has come to the fore in many different contexts and catches the imagination of people inside and outside the churches. In this situation we have come to discern anew that reconciliation is at the heart of Christian faith. This takes place both in ecumenical and evangelical mission thinking. The reconciling love of God shown in Jesus Christ is an important biblical theme and a central element in the life and ministry of the church. We affirm thus now that the Holy Spirit calls us to a ministry of reconciliation and to express this in both the spirituality and strategies of our mission and evangelism.

2. There are a number of other reasons why reconciliation has become so prominent in the world today. These are related to the contemporary trends of globalization, post-modernity and fragmentation as identified in the CWME study document "Mission and Evangelism in Unity Today" (2000).[2] Globalization has brought different communities of the world into closer contact than ever before and has highlighted human commonality. At the same time it has exposed the diversity of interests and worldviews among different groups. On the one hand, there are new ways to express unity and cross the boundaries that have divided us. On the other hand, there are also clashes of cultures, reli-

gions, economic interests and genders, which leave a legacy of hurt and grievances. The heightened enmity that has resulted from globalization and the imbalance of power in today's world has been strikingly confirmed in the terrorist acts of September 11, 2001 and the subsequent "war on terror". In this context also, a number of initiatives, both by civil society and by churches, have contributed to the reconstruction of societies after conflict through processes of truth and reconciliation. Christian witnesses are called upon to help bring peace with justice in situations of tension, violence, and conflict. As the churches seek reconciliation and peace, the World Council of Churches has launched the Decade to Overcome Violence (2001-2010).

3. The dominance and pervasiveness of global market forces have led to enormous changes in the way people live and work, yet economic globalization is highly ambiguous. While free trade and competition have led to economic growth and increased prosperity in some countries, particularly in Asia, the economic policies of the richer nations have had tremendous and often highly damaging effects on poorer nations. More are victims rather than beneficiaries. Unfair trade laws protect the richer nations and exclude and exploit the poorer ones. Many of the poorer countries are saddled with debt and its repayment is an intolerable burden. Structural adjustment programmes imposed by global bodies pay little regard to local wisdom and it is the poor who suffer most under them. In this situation, the Jubilee Debt Campaign has had a significant effect in raising awareness of trade imbalance and influencing G8 decisions. True reconciliation that involves the repentance of the rich and brings justice for the poor is urgently needed.

4. The network of global communications also brings benefit to some and excludes others. In some respects, by increasing the possibilities of dialogue and cooperation, it is beneficial in widening fellowship and facilitating alternative movements for change. However, the mass culture of post-modernity spread in this way is often experienced as a threat to personal and nation-

al identities and contributes to the increasing fragmentation of societies. As a result of globalization, many have lost their family and local roots, many have been displaced by migration, and exclusion is widely experienced. Many are longing for the embrace of others and sense a need for belonging and community. In this situation, we are called to be reconciling and healing communities.

5. We look to the Holy Spirit, who in the Bible is related with communion (2 Cor 13:13), to lead us and all creation in integrity and wholeness towards reconciliation with God and one another. However, exposed to the strength and vicissitudes of global forces, the difficulties of discerning the Holy Spirit among the complexities of the world have never been greater as we are faced with difficult personal and strategic choices in mission. In 1996, at the last WCC conference on mission and evangelism, we were reminded in Salvador, Bahía, Brazil, how the perpetrators of economic injustice denied the rights of Indigenous populations and plundered resources given by the Creator for all. We asked for forgiveness for this and sought reconciliation.[3] Affirming that "the Spirit poured out on the day of Pentecost makes all cultures worthy vehicles of God's love" and "enables a real awakening of the image of God" in persons in oppressed groups, we committed ourselves at Salvador to "the search for alternative models of community, more equitable economic systems, fair trade practices, responsible use of the media, and just environmental practice".[4]

6. All over the world, we are experiencing a thirst for spiritual experience, a renewal within religions, a resurgence of fundamentalist forms of religiosity, as well as a proliferation of new religious movements. All this is linked to the influence of globalization and post-modernity. On the one hand, the variety of spiritualities to which we are exposed raises our spiritual awareness, enriches our perception of God's mystery and broadens our horizons. On the other, we also discern increasing tensions between religions which are due to many internal and external

factors, in particular religious reinforcement of closed identities, justification of violence and aggressive methods of religious propagation. These trends make it even more urgent for us to seek a reconciliatory spirituality for mission.

7. Within the Christian faith, while some churches continue to decline, many are experiencing rapid numerical growth. The centre of gravity of Christianity has decisively shifted towards the poorer nations of the world and the faith is widely expressed in a Pentecostal-charismatic form. The rapid growth of the Pentecostal and charismatic churches is a noticeable fact of our time. The positive impact of charismatic experience gives great encouragement and hope for the future of Christian faith. It calls our attention to the theology of the Holy Spirit and the way in which the Spirit repeatedly renews the church for its mission in every age. At the same time, the potential for tension and disunity reminds us of the Spirit's close association with reconciliation and peace. It is important that this pneumatological orientation should never take the form of a "pneumatomonism", as in the past when a hidden "christomonism" relegated the Holy Spirit into an ancillary role. In the mission of the church the understanding of Christology should always be conditioned in a constitutive way by pneumatology.

8. Since Pentecost the Holy Spirit has inspired the church to proclaim Jesus Christ as the Lord and Saviour and we continue to be obedient to the command to preach the gospel in all the world. The Holy Spirit anointed the Son of God to "preach good news to the poor, heal the broken-hearted, proclaim liberty to captives, recovery of sight to the blind and set at liberty those who are oppressed" (Luke 4:18). We seek to continue his liberating and healing mission. This involves bold proclamation of the liberating gospel to people bound by sin, a healing ministry to the sick and suffering, and the struggle for justice on the side of the oppressed and marginalized. Recognizing that the Spirit of God has been present in creation since the beginning and goes before us in our mission and evangelism, we have also affirmed

the Spirit's creativity expressed in diverse cultures and we have entered into dialogue with people of other faiths. Now, confronted with the world situation we have described, we are rediscovering the ministry of the Spirit to reconcile and to heal.

2. The triune God, source and initiator of reconciliation: biblical, theological and liturgical perspectives

9. Reconciliation is the work of the triune God bringing fulfilment to God's eternal purposes of creation and salvation through Jesus Christ: "For in him all the fullness of God was pleased to dwell, and through him to reconcile to himself all things, whether on earth or in heaven, making peace by the blood of his cross... For in him the whole fullness of deity dwells bodily" (Col. 1:19-20, 2:9). In the person of Jesus Christ the divine nature and the human nature were reconciled, united forever. This is the starting point for our reconciliation with God. We have to actualize by God's grace and our efforts what we already have in Christ, through the Holy Spirit.

The Godhead, the Three-in-One, expresses the very nature of community, the reconciliation we hope for: "The Trinity, the source and image of our existence, shows the importance of diversity, otherness and intrinsic relationships in constituting a community".[5]

Reconciliation from a biblical perspective

10. The Bible is full of stories of reconciliation. The Old Testament tells a number of stories of conflict and strife between brothers, family members, peoples; some of these end in reconciliation and others are unresolved. It acknowledges and bemoans the dimension of violence and underlines the need for and the power of reconciliation. The family stories of Jacob and Esau (Gen. 25:19-33:20), or of Joseph and his brothers (Gen. 37-45) are examples for interpersonal - and perhaps also communal - conflicts. They also illustrate the power of reconciling attitudes of people who try to solve strife, enmity, and experi-

ences or perceptions of injustice through negotiations, repentance, forgiveness, and searching for a common basis and a shared future. The Old Testament addresses again and again the estrangement between God and God's people and God's desire and urge for reconciliation and restoration of a relationship that was broken and fragmented through human pride and various forms of rebellion against the God of life and justice. Reconciliation is thus very much a theme in the biblical narratives and in the liturgical language of Israel - such as the Psalms, even though the Hebrew language does not know the specific term "reconciliation". In the books of the lament tradition, such as Lamentations and Job, human longing for reconciliation with God is poignantly expressed.

11. Similarly in the New Testament, though the actual term "reconciliation" does not appear very prominently, the matter itself is prevalent throughout. John's gospel shows a particular concern for truth and peace; in the gospel of Luke salvation is closely linked to the healing ministry of Jesus. The Book of Acts tells how Jews and Gentiles were reconciled in one new community. And throughout his letters, Paul is greatly concerned that those whom Christ has reconciled in his body should not be divided and that community life should be the first expression of God's plan to reconcile all things. He envisages the unity of not only Jew and Gentile but also of slave and free, male and female in Christ (Gal. 3:28).

12. Apart from Matthew 5:24, where it relates to the reconciliation of individuals, we find the terms "reconciliation" and "to reconcile" - the Greek words are *katallage/katallassein* - only in the letters of the apostle Paul (2 Cor. 5:17-20; Rom. 5:10-11, 11:15; 1 Cor. 7:11, and then Eph. 2:16 and Col. 1:20-22). However, the apostle expresses the theme so forcefully that it emerges as a key notion in the Christian identity as a whole. Paul uses the term reconciliation in exploring the nature of God, to illumine the content of the gospel as good news, and to explain the ministry and mission of the apostle and the church in

the world. The term "reconciliation" thus becomes an almost all-embracing term to articulate what is at the heart of the Christian faith.

There are several features of reconciliation as used by Paul to note briefly:

13. The very notion of reconciliation presupposes the experience of broken communion. This may be in the form of estrangement, separation, enmity, hatred, exclusion, fragmentation, distorted relationships. It usually also encompasses a certain degree of injustice, harm and suffering. Reconciliation, in biblical as well as secular language, is understood as the effort towards and engagement for mending this broken and distorted relationship and building up community and relationships afresh.

14. Paul applies the notion of reconciliation to three different though overlapping realms of brokenness and hostility, in which healing of relationship occurs: reconciliation between God and human beings; reconciliation of different groups of human beings; and reconciliation of the cosmos.

15. Reconciliation is much more than simply a superficial fixing of distortions, the arrival of a status quo of coexistence. Reconciliation looks at a transformation of the present, a very deep-rooted renewal. The "peace" which Paul speaks about is first and foremost peace with God (cf. Rom. 5:1,11). It is also in a prominent way the transformation of human relationships and the building of a community: It is the radical new peace between Jews and Gentiles that results from Christ breaking down the wall of hostility (Eph. 2:14). It is the transformation of the whole creation towards peace as it is expressed in Colossians 1:20, where Paul speaks of Christ as reconciling "all things, whether on earth or in heaven, making peace by the blood of his cross". The last reference indicates that reconciliation envisions a new creation as Paul expresses so vividly in 2 Corinthians 5:17. The category of "new creation" shows that there is even more in view than a mending of brokenness. Reconciliation is a

totally new quality of being, as expressed in the hymn celebrating the gathering of all things in Christ (Eph. 1:10).

16. According to Paul, it is God who takes the initiative towards reconciliation. Furthermore, God has already achieved reconciliation for the world: "In Christ God was reconciling the world to himself" (2 Cor. 5:19). Human beings may seek for reconciliation and minister reconciliation but the initiative and the effectiveness of reconciliation lies with God. Human beings are only recipients of the gift of reconciliation. It is therefore essential to affirm that Christian life and attitude is grounded in the experience of reconciliation through Godself. Christians discover what God has already done in Christ.

17. The human predicament that creates the need for reconciliation with God is the alienation from God that is due to human sin, disobedience to and break of communion with God, resulting in guilt and death, both spiritually and physically (Rom. 3:23; Eph. 2:1-3) This enmity between God and human beings was overcome through the death of Jesus on the cross. "When we were enemies we were reconciled to God through the death of his Son" (Rom. 5:10). On the cross the Son of God freely gave his life as an atoning sacrifice for the sins and guilt of the whole world. He is the lamb of God who carries the sins of the world (John 1:29), who himself "bore our sins in his own body on the tree" (1 Pet. 2:24). Through Christ's substitutionary death "for us" (Rom. 5:8; Gal. 1:4) reconciliation has been achieved once for all leading to forgiveness of sins, communion with God and new life in God's kingdom. This is all by the grace and love of God.

18. The Christian narrative of reconciliation is thus based on and centred in the story of the incarnation, passion, death, resurrection and ascension of Jesus Christ. The messianic ministry of Jesus of Nazareth links his suffering with the suffering of all humanity, and is therefore an expression of the deep solidarity of God with an agonized, fragmented and tortured world. The cross is, at the same time, an expression of the divine protest

against this suffering, for Jesus of Nazareth suffered as the innocent victim. He refused to take refuge in violence, he persisted in the love of his enemies and he made love towards God and his fellow-human beings the central concern of his life. The gruesome act of throwing "the one who was just" out of this world is in itself the judgment of a world in which the powerful seem to prevail over the victims. In Christ, through whose wounds we are healed (1 Pet. 2:24), we also experience God seeking to rectify the wrongs of this world through the power of love with which God, in his Son, gave himself up for others, even for the perpetrators of violence and injustice.

19. The cross of Christ, and the obligation of the Christians to participate in the suffering of the people and their struggle for a better life, which results from it, is not the only criterion for the mission of the church. It is through the resurrection that the death of Christ receives its true meaning. The resurrection means that God himself recognized Jesus and his cross; it was a liberating judgment making the cross an instrument of salvation and reconciliation. The resurrection is even more, however, being itself an integral part of God's reconciling work in Christ. For Christians resurrection is not understood as just an historical event of the past, nor just an article of faith, but also a mystically lived present-day reality. In missiology, cross and resurrection form an indissoluble unity. The church exists not only because Christ died on the cross, but also and primarily because he is risen from the dead, thus becoming the first fruit of all humanity (cf. 1 Cor. 15:20). The centrality of resurrection in both the NT and the life of the church not only gives "the hope that is in us" (1 Pet. 3:15), but it inevitably leads to the primary importance of eschatology.

20. It is through the Holy Spirit that human beings are empowered to share in the narrative of God reconciling the world in Jesus Christ. In Romans 5, where Paul explores the way God reconciles sinners and even God's enemies and the ungodly with Godself, Paul says that the love of God has been poured out into

our hearts through the Holy Spirit. In Jesus Christ, who was raised and ascended into heaven, we not only enjoy the gift of reconciliation, we are also sent in service and ministry into the world. This is expressed, for example, in the ethical teaching of Paul where he urged individuals and communities to be signs and expressions of the reconciliation they had experienced (cf. Rom. 12:9-21). It is also expressed in the way Paul talks about his own mission as a "ministry of reconciliation" (2 Cor. 5:18). To share in this ministry of reconciliation - that is to participate in the Holy Spirit's work of reconciliation and communicate God's reconciling activity to all of humanity - is the Christian calling today as much as in Paul's day.

21. This means that God's work of reconciliation with human beings was not finished on the cross and in the resurrection; it goes on through history in the ministry of reconciliation that has been entrusted to the church. Based on the reconciliation effected in Christ's death and resurrection and on God's behalf, the church challenges and invites all people to be reconciled with God. "Now all things are of God, who has reconciled us to himself and given us the ministry of reconciliation" (2 Cor. 5:18-21) This offer of reconciliation is received and becomes a personal reality through faith (Eph. 2:8).

The Holy Spirit and reconciliation

22. The Holy Spirit empowers the church to participate in this work of reconciliation as the document "Mission and Evangelism in Unity" states: "The mission of God (*missio Dei*) is the source of and basis for the mission of the church, the body of Christ. Through Christ in the Holy Spirit, God indwells the church, empowering and energizing its members."[6] The ministry of the Spirit (2 Cor. 3:8) is a ministry of reconciliation, made possible through Christ and entrusted to us (2 Cor. 5:18-19).

23. In the power of the Spirit, the church as koinonia - the communion of the Holy Spirit (2 Cor. 13:13) - continually grows into a healing and reconciling community that shares the joys

and sorrows of her members and reaches out to those in need of forgiveness and reconciliation. According to the Book of Acts (2:44-45, 4:32-37), the early church, having been born on the day of Pentecost, shared her goods among her members, pointing to the inter-relatedness of "spiritual" and "material" concerns in Christian mission and church life. One aspect of the empowering ministry of the Holy Spirit is to endow Christians and Christian communities with charismatic gifts, which include healing (1 Cor. 12:9; Acts 3).

24. The church herself is in need of continuing renewal by the Spirit to be able to discern the mind of Christ as well as be convicted by the Spirit of division and sin within (John 16:8-11). This repentance within the church of Christ is itself part of the ministry and witness of reconciliation to the world.

25. The Holy Spirit blows where the Spirit wills (cf. John 3:8). Thus, the Spirit knows no limits and reaches out to people of all faiths as well as those without any religious commitment - a growing number in this time of secularization. The church is called to discern the signs of the Spirit in the world and witness to Christ in the power of the Spirit (Acts 1:8) as well as be engaged in all forms of liberation and reconciliation (2 Cor. 5:18-19).

26. In the sufferings of the present time, the Spirit shares our "groans" and the childbirth pains of the whole of creation subjected to "bondage under decay" (Rom. 8:26,21-22). Therefore, we are looking forward to the redemption of our bodies (Rom. 8:23) with hope and joy. The same Spirit of God that "swept over the face of the waters" (Gen. 1:2) in creation now indwells the church and works in the world often in mysterious and unknown ways. The Spirit will participate in the ushering in of the new creation when God finally will be all in all.

27. Since the time of the New Testament, two understandings of pneumatology can be discerned. One emphasizes the Holy Spirit as fully dependant on Christ, as being the agent of Christ to fulfill the task of mission, and has led to a missiology focusing on

sending and *going forth*. The other understands the Holy Spirit as the source of Christ, and the church as the eschatological synaxis (coming together) of the people of God in God's kingdom. In that second perspective, mission as going forth is the outcome, not the origin of the church. Mission is the liturgy *after* the Liturgy. Because reconciliation is a prerequisite of the eucharist (the act that actually constitutes the church) it becomes a primary of mission in that perspective.

Liturgical perspectives on reconciliation

28. The church's mission, in the power of the Spirit, derives from the teaching, life and work of our Lord Jesus Christ. This is to be understood in reference to the expectations of Judaism. The core of this was the idea of the coming of a Messiah, who in the "last days" of history would establish his kingdom (Joel 3:1; Isa. 2:2, 59:21; Ezek. 36:24, etc.) by calling all the dispersed and afflicted people of God *into one place*, reconciled to God and becoming one body united around him (Mic. 4:1-4; Isa. 2:2-4; Ps. 147:2-3). In the gospel of John it is clearly stated that the high priest "prophesied that Jesus should die... not for the nation only, but to *gather into one* the children of God who are scattered abroad" (John 11:51-52).

29. This reconciliation was experienced in the liturgical, more precisely "eucharistic" (in the wider sense), life of the early church. The early Christian community suffered from factions and divisions but, reconciled through the grace of our Lord to God, felt obliged to extend horizontally this reconciliation to one another by being incorporated into the one people of God through the eucharist, a significant act of identity, which was celebrated as a manifestation (more precisely a foretaste) of the coming kingdom. It is not accidental that the condition for participating in the Lord's table was, and still often is, an act of reconciliation with one's sisters and brothers which bears profound symbolic value and is remindful of the core of the gospel (Matt. 5:23-24). By sharing the "kiss of love", church members give each other a sign of reconciliation and commit themselves to the

healing of relationships in the community. In a related manner, Paul challenges the Corinthians to take seriously the fact that their failure to share could jeopardize the very celebration of the Lord's supper (1 Cor. 11:20-21).

30. This eucharistic act is not the only liturgical rite of reconciliation in the healing process. Baptism, which presupposes an act of repentance, is a common sign of incorporation through the Spirit into the one body (1 Cor. 12:13; Eph. 4:4-5). The act of confession, which has sacramental significance for some churches, was originally meant as the necessary reconciling process with the community - a sacrament of reconciliation. There is also the act - or sacrament - of anointment for healing. For many churches the Lord's supper itself also has therapeutic meaning. These examples draw our attention to the importance of reconciliation and healing in the life and mission of the church.

31. These manifestations of the kingdom in the community were the starting point of Christian mission, the springboard of the church's witnessing exodus to the world. The missiological imperatives of the church stem exactly from this awareness of the church as a dynamic and corporate body of reconciled believers commissioned to witness to the coming kingdom of God. In striving to manifest the ministry of reconciliation (2 Cor. 5:18ff.) to the world, we become a reconciling community. This ministry to be "ambassadors for Christ" includes a commitment to the proclamation of the gospel: "We entreat you on behalf of Christ, be reconciled to God. For our sake he made him to be sin who knew no sin, so that in him we might become the righteousness of God" (2 Cor. 5:20-21).

In ecumenical perspective such evangelism "aims to build up a reconciling and reconciled community (cf. 2 Cor. 5:19) that will point to the fullness of God's reign, which is 'righteousness and peace and joy in the Holy Spirit' (Rom. 14:17)". This affirmation of the preparatory document for Salvador finds an echo in the recent WCC mission statement: "To speak of evangelism means to emphasise the proclamation of God's offer of freedom and reconciliation, together with the invitation to join those who follow Christ and work for the reign of God."[7]

3. Reconciliation as an imperative for mission

32. The powerful convergence of a new interest in reconciliation and healing within the churches, and a parallel new quest for healing and reconciliation in many societies around the world, have prompted us to rethink what God is calling us to in mission today. Remembering that the reconciliation we have received in Jesus Christ is to be shared in the world, we have come to see reconciliation as part of mission.

33. Mission as ministry of reconciliation involves the obligation to share the gospel of Jesus Christ in all its fullness, the good news of him who through his incarnation, death and resurrection has once for all provided the basis for reconciliation with God, forgiveness of sins and new life in the power of the Holy Spirit. This ministry invites people to accept God's offer of reconciliation in Christ, and to become his disciples in the communion of his church. It promises the hope of fullness of life in God, both in this age and in God's future, eternal kingdom.

34. The ministry of reconciliation also involves the work for reconciliation among persons and societies. In order to understand what this participation in God's mission of reconciliation may mean, we will focus upon the goals and processes of reconciliation and healing. This involves both some general thoughts and reflections upon the dynamics of how reconciliation and healing come about.

35. Reconciliation is and results from a process leading to peace with justice. The vision is to establish community, where brokenness and sectarianism are overcome and people live together with mutual respect and tolerance. Reconciliation results in communication with one another without fear. It implies tolerance of others, inclusion and consideration of them. Reconciled

community is where differences can be resolved through dialogue and without resort to violence.

36. Reconciliation is sought between *individuals*, in order to overcome divisions, enmity and conflicts from the past. Here the internal dynamics for both parties, for victims and wrongdoers must be explored. Reconciliation also needs to occur between *groups or communities*. In these instances social and structural relations will need special attention. And reconciliation sometimes needs to happen within and among *nations*, in which the whole structures of societies will need examination. In the first instance, between individuals, reconciliation is often about restoring dignity and a sense of humanity. In the second instance, reconciliation focuses upon how to live together, both as human beings and in the whole of creation. In the third instance, on national levels, the institutions of society itself will need attention for reconstruction to be possible.

37. Reconciliation is both a *goal* and a *process*. As individuals and societies we need a vision to keep us moving towards a future state of peace and well-being. But without understanding the process we can lose heart and sense of direction in our work. In actual practice, we will find ourselves moving back and forth between goal and process, since we need both in reconciliation and healing.

Dynamics of reconciliation processes

38. Attention needs to be given both to initiating the process of reconciliation and to sustaining it. The participants in this process are often divided into *victims* and *wrongdoers*. The two parties are easily distinguished and identified, for example in many cases of victims of rape and those who perpetrate the act. But in extended conflicts, victims may, at a later date, become wrongdoers, and wrongdoers become victims. This makes clear-cut categories less helpful. While Christian practice has special regard for the plight of victims, reconciliation and healing require restoration and healing both of the victim and repentance and transformation of the wrongdoer. These things do not

always happen in a clear sequence, but becoming a "new creation" (2 Cor. 5:17) requires change in both.

39. Six aspects of the reconciliation and healing process need special attention. They are: **truth, memory, repentance, justice, forgiveness and love.**

Establishing the **truth** about the past is often difficult because abuses and atrocities have been shrouded in silence. Healing requires that the silence be broken and the truth be allowed to come to light. It allows for recognition of what has been hidden.

40. At other times, under a repressive regime for instance, there has been a systematic distortion of the truth. Lies prevail where truth should dwell. In such cases, the truth needs to be asserted. This is especially true when the language of reconciliation itself is misused. There have been instances where wrongdoers have called for "reconciliation" when they really mean that victims should ignore the wrongdoing done, and life should continue as though nothing happened. In such cases, the meaning of the word "reconciliation" has been so poisoned that it cannot even be used. In other cases, wrongdoers urge hasty "reconciliation" so that the claims of the victims will not even be considered. They may do this by making Christians feel guilty for not being able to forgive quickly. Such false uses of the idea of reconciliation must be resisted.

41. At a national level, after prolonged conflict and struggle, truth and reconciliation commissions have been established to seek out the truth about the past. The Commission in South Africa is perhaps the most well-known. The need for such commissions underscores how difficult it is to establish the truth, and how important it is for reconciliation and healing.

42. The Christian understanding of truth can help in such situations. The Spirit of God is the Spirit of truth (John 14:17), and Jesus "who is the way, and the truth, and the life" (John 14:6) prayed that his disciples be sanctified by the Spirit of truth (John 17:17). Establishing the truth, especially after situations of con-

flict, can be difficult. Respect for the truth comes from knowing God wants the truth to be told (cf. the prophetic tradition).

43. **Memory** is closely linked to truth. How will the past be remembered, how shall we speak of it? Authentic memory should yield the truth about the past. Traumatic memories of acts of wrongdoing or atrocity often will need healing if they are to be the building blocks of a different kind of future. To heal memories means that they lose their toxic quality. When that happens, memories do not hold us hostage to the past, but empower us to create a future where the wrongdoing of the past cannot happen again.

44. Memories are not just about the past. They are the basis for identity. *How* we remember the past is both the basis for how we will live and relate to one another in the present, and how we will envision the future. For that reason, memory is central to the process of reconciliation and healing.

45. Memories that do not heal can inhibit reconciliation. Sometimes the healing takes more than a generation. In some instances victims are so submerged in their memories that they need help in coming free of them. This may imply to provide a space for the victims to express their anger. In a few instances, victims do not want to be healed, and use their memories to keep any progress from happening. Accompanying victims so that they can come free from traumatic memories is an important task of those who work for reconciliation.

46. Projects of recovering memory that has been suppressed or distorted are often important for building a different future together. Publishing the results of Truth and Reconciliation Commissions,[8] or collecting recollections of what happened,[9] are examples of this. Recovering memory can also be a threat to the wrongdoers who still hold power.[10]

47. Recovering memory and allowing it to help us live in the present, as well as imagine the future, is central to Christian practice and witness. We celebrate the eucharist to remember what happened to Jesus: his betrayal, suffering and death, and

how he was raised from the dead. It is the memory of what God has done in the story of Jesus that gives us hope and the Spirit of Christ who empowers us in our work of reconciliation.

48. In many cases of conflict there is a need for **repentance** (metanoia) before reconciliation can take place. Because there may be a situation of wrongdoing and guilt, personal or collective, that has caused the enmity or estrangement, true reconciliation cannot take place until the guilty part has repented of sin and wrongdoing. Jesus' proclamation of the kingdom of God was accompanied by a call for repentance and faith in the gospel (Mark 1:15). It is noteworthy that Jesus' call for repentance is motivated by the new time of salvation that is inaugurated by his coming. True repentance cannot be the result of threats and fear, but has to come from a realization of guilt and a hope for a new reconciled relationship based on forgiveness (cf. Acts 2:38).

49. **Justice** is essential to the work of reconciliation. Three kinds of justice are needed. First, there is **retributive justice**, where wrongdoers are held accountable for their actions. This is important both for acknowledging that wrong has been done, and as a statement that such wrongdoing will not be tolerated in the future. Retributive justice should be the task of the legally constituted state. Punishment outside that forum can be renegade action or sheer revenge, and should be avoided. If the state itself is implicated in the corruption, it may be possible to achieve retributive justice by means of non-violent protest.[11] This will require great personal sacrifice.

50. Second, there is **restorative justice**, in which what has been taken wrongfully from victims is restored, either directly or in some symbolic way. This may be by reparation or compensation. In Luke's gospel, the story of Zacchaeus's encounter with Jesus (19:1-10) shows how an authentic repentance resulting from meeting Christ can lead to a radical form of restitution. In other cases, for example when the perpetrator or victim has died, some other statement of reconciliation may need to be found - such as a public memorial.

51. And finally, there is **structural justice**, whereby the institutions of society are reformed to prevent instances of injustice from happening in the future. Dimensions of restorative and structural justice often need special attention. For example, to achieve economic justice, reform of global trade laws and the mechanisms of trade will be necessary. Gender justice will require the special contributions of women to overcoming injustice and retaining right relations. To overcome sexism and racism structural reform will be necessary. In recent years, the need for ecological justice has come to the fore as well.

52. The Holy Spirit spoke through the prophets of old against injustice and anointed Jesus Christ to bring freedom to the oppressed (Luke 4:18-19). The Spirit gives gifts of prophecy and boldness today as Christians struggle especially to aid in the process of restorative justice, and work towards the reforms that structural justice require. Biblical images of covenant - care for all, and right relations between God and humanity - support efforts for these reforms of society. These are illustrated by the collection from the churches taken up by the apostle Paul to Jerusalem so that there might be "equality" between the churches in the mutual meeting of one another's needs (2 Cor. 8:14).

53. **Forgiveness** is often considered a specifically religious dimension of reconciling and healing. It is important to realize that forgiveness does not mean condoning past wrongdoing, or even foregoing punishment. Forgiveness acknowledges the past, but seeks a different relationship both to the wrongdoer and to the deed. Without forgiveness, we remain locked in our relationships to the past and cannot have a different kind of future.

54. Along with having a Christian vision of the whole, seeking reconciliation for the human community today requires interaction with the different communities of faith. For us as Christians, this will call for some knowledge of how the other great religious traditions envision healing and wholeness, since many situations will require our acting together. In those situations also, we as Christians must be able to communicate our

own contribution to the common task. Many cultures have their own spiritual and ritual resources for bringing about reconciliation and healing. Whenever possible, these need to be incorporated into our work towards reconciliation.

55. Forgiveness has special import for Christians. We believe that it is God who forgives sin (Mark 2:7-12). Jesus came among us preaching the forgiveness of sins (Luke 24:47), pointing to the graciousness of God and the possibility of overcoming the past for the sake of a different kind of future. Personal experience of acceptance and grace can be life-changing, inspiring individuals to reach out in love to others and transform society, as the story of Zacchaeus illustrates. After his resurrection, when he breathed the Holy Spirit into his disciples, Jesus sent them out with a ministry of forgiveness (John 20:21-23).

56. Forgiveness by God is bound up with our willingness to forgive others (see Matt. 6:12,14-15). Because of this, Christians often say that we should "forgive and forget". We can never forget wrongdoing, as though it never happened. To ask victims to do this would be to demean them once again. We can never forget, but we can remember in a different way - a way that allows for a different relationship to the past and to the wrongdoer. That is what we are called to as Christians.

57. **Love** (agape) is the most characteristic feature of Christianity. The triune God, the Three-in-One expresses the perfect union of distinct persons, the supreme love, which encompasses everything. God reveals and manifests Godself as love, because God is love (John 3:16; 1 John 4:7-21). Being created according to God's image and recreated through baptism, God's love "has been poured into our hearts through the Holy Spirit which has been given to us" (Rom. 5:5; cf. Gal. 5:22). That is why the commandment to love our enemies (Matt. 5:44) is not a commandment that is impossible to fulfill. God never asks from us what God did not give already. To love the enemies is simultaneously God's gift and the human personal contribu-

tion, "the more excellent way" (1 Cor. 12:31, 13:1-8) which brings us to a holy life, to conformity with Christ, our model (Gal. 4:19), to his way of being and thinking: "We have the mind of Christ" (1 Cor. 2:16). Love encompasses the whole process of reconciliation as the very sign of its authenticity.

58. Truth, memory, repentance, justice, forgiveness and love are important and essential elements for holistic complete and true reconciliation. Experience has shown that reconciliation is **not always complete**. Most of the stories told in the Bible are not stories of full reconciliation. The well-known stories of Sarah and Hagar, Jacob and Esau, Rachel and Leah, leave us wondering whether the characters were truly reconciled. Even the parable of the prodigal son makes no mention of the reconciliation between the two brothers. Most situations of intense conflict result in some reservations on either side that hinder complete acceptance and reconciliation. This is not to suggest that true reconciliation cannot take place, but rather to acknowledge that the reconciliatory process can take long, perhaps even a lifetime or longer, for the eradication of hurt, suspicion and anger.

59. Another dimension of this is that the perpetrator of conflict may never repent or seek forgiveness even after the period of conflict. Stories from South Africa and several other parts of the world attest to this fact. In such instances, victims may have to find ways to cope with the situation by moving away from the site of oppression, a form of resistance. The victim then often realizes that forgiveness may have to be given even when repentance is not forthcoming nor forgiveness sought by the perpetrator. The victim however must become able to live on and cope with the situation. Carrying feelings of anger, hurt and bitterness is detrimental to the self and growth of the individual or community. There are other situations where the perpetrator is really seeking forgiveness, but does not receive it. In such cases, the perpetrator is the one who must find other ways to resolve his or her guilt. In can also happen that the victim needs to forgive him- or herself for having allowed something to happen and for having shown complicity in systems of oppression. It is impor-

tant that such dimensions of the perpetrator's or victim's experience be duly considered in the dynamics of reconciliation.

60. Whether at social, community or personal level reconciliation and healing are goals we seek within the ambivalence and brokenness of human existence. These goals are inspired by the biblical vision of the eschatological restoration of the *original shalom, the promised final realization of the kingdom of God*, when all will have been healed, made whole again and united in God. In contemporary human history, we may hope to reach levels of reconciliation or healing, or justice, peace and the integrity of creation. Whereas the vision of full reconciliation and healing embraces the totality of God's creation, our contribution is limited as is our vision. But we are called to give corporate signs of God's reconciliation, for in so doing we renew hope. Indeed, seeking reconciliation and healing in our world requires a constant moving back and forth between imagining reconciliation within human life, society and creation as a goal and as the process of reaching that goal. This may be a long and difficult struggle and it cannot be carried through unless it is in a spirit of love that "bears all things, believes all things, hopes all things, endures all things" (1 Cor. 13:7). In the process we do not lose hope and, at the same time, focus our participation in the reconciling and healing work of the Holy Spirit in the whole creation.

4. The reconciling mission of the church

61. The Holy Spirit transforms the church and empowers it to be missional: "The Holy Spirit transforms Christians into living, courageous and bold witnesses (cf. Acts 1:8)."[12]   Therefore, for the church, mission is not an option but an imperative: "Mission is central to Christian faith and theology. It is not an option but is rather an existential calling and vocation. Mission is constitutive of and conditions the very being of the church and of all Christians." The church is by nature called to participate in God's mission: "Through Christ in the Holy Spirit... participating in God's mission... should be natural for all Christians and all churches"[13] (cf. the reference to the priestly ministry of the community in 1 Pet. 2:2-12).

62. The church's mission in the power of the Spirit is to work for reconciliation and healing in the context of brokenness. Reconciliation constitutes an important focus and characteristic of the mission of God which bears consequences for the church's mission: "The church is sent into the world to reconcile humanity and renew creation by calling people and nations to repentance, announcing forgiveness of sin and a new beginning in relations with God and with neighbours through Jesus Christ."[14] We expect full reconciliation as the establishment of shalom by God at the end of time that is the creation - or re-creation - of harmonious and just relationships. It is a holistic process, initiated by God and extended to the whole creation, both human and non-human. As we and all creation struggle for freedom from our bondage to decay, "the Spirit helps us in our weakness... [and] intercedes for us with sighs too deep for words" (Rom. 8:22-26). In a context of broken relationships in the world today, the specific challenge for the church is to grasp more deeply the gift of God's reconciliation in its life and ministry on behalf of the whole created order.

Reconciliation in the context of brokenness

63. The primary broken relationship is between *God* and humanity. The gospel of reconciliation is a call to turn to God, to be converted to God and to renew our faith in the One who constantly invites us to be in communion with Godself, with one another and with the whole creation. We rejoice that through our Saviour Jesus Christ, this reconciliation has been made possible: "Through our Lord Jesus Christ we have now received our reconciliation" (Rom. 5:11). We are called to extend this reconciliation to the rest of the world in mission and to join our energies with that of the Spirit of God in creation.

64. At the heart of the brokenness today is the distortion and destruction of the integral bond that existed in the divine order, between humanity and the rest of *creation*. The human-centred separation of human and non-human creation has led to a ten-

dency of some parts of humanity to conquer and destroy nature. Much of the ecological crisis we face today may be attributed to a lack of respect for life and the integrity of creation. An ecological healing - or "ecociliation" - is what Christians envisage: the reconciliation of "all things, whether on earth or in heaven" (Col. 1:20). In the Nicene-Constantinopolitan Creed we confess the Holy Spirit as the lord and the giver of life. Mission in the Spirit warrants a new perspective - a life-centred approach that will cause the earth to flourish and sustain human communities. This model of cosmic reconciliation and healing provides a powerful basis for reconciliation among humanity.

65. Brokenness is also felt in the area of *human relationships*. The image of God is distorted in estrangement and enmity, which is often related to power structures. These are manifested concretely in manyfold forms of discrimination in the world at large on the bases of caste, race, gender, religion, sexual orientation, and socio-economic status. Mission in terms of reconciliation and healing in this context is about going beyond and transcending such frontiers and thereby restoring the consciousness of the image of God in humanity. In real terms, the mission of the churches is to strive to work in common for the dismantling of divisive walls - those within the church as well as outside. This means taking part in ecumenical attempts at reconciliation within and among churches and in people's struggles for reconstruction of society on the basis of justice and human rights, as well as providing a space for dialogue and debate where society or the churches remain profoundly divided. The body of Christ is endowed with various spiritual gifts (1 Cor. 12:8-10; see also Rom. 12:6-8). Exercised in the spirit of love (1 Cor. 13:1-3; Rom. 12:9-10), these build up the community and express its reconciled unity in diversity.

66. In a context where there are victims and perpetrators of injustice and exploitation, the church has a particular missionary role to play, namely that of a *bridge-builder*, between the poor and the rich, women and men, black and white, and so on. The

Holy Spirit has been described as "the Go-Between God"[15] because of the Spirit's role in creating and sustaining communion (Eph. 2:18, 4:3). The "go-between" or "in-between" position is not be construed as a value-neutral position but acknowledged as a rather risky and costly position to be in. While taking the sides of the victims, the church also has the mission of reaching out to the victimizers with the challenges of the gospel. Mission at the point of "in-betweenness" is simultaneously a mission of empowering the powerless by accompanying them and also of challenging the perpetrators of hurt to repent. In this way it becomes a mission of mutual life-giving.

67. Brokenness is also sadly a mark of today's *church*. The divisions among churches, both doctrinal and non-theological, are a challenge to the mission of reconciliation and healing. A divided church is an aberration of the body of Christ (1 Cor. 1:13) and grieves the Holy Spirit (Eph. 4:25-32). If churches are not able to reconcile one with the other, they are failing the gospel call and will lack credibility in witness. "Sent to a world in need of unity and greater interdependence amidst the competition and fragmentation of the human community, the church is called to be sign and instrument of God's reconciling love... Divisions among Christians are a counter-witness to Christ and contradict their witness to reconciliation in Christ."[16] There has been a particular tendency of churches and Christian movements to split in and over mission work during the last century. Competition and conflict in mission, in development or interchurch aid, as well as proselytism, have proved to be a serious counter-witness to Christ's reconciling work. Christians and churches are called to undertake or strengthen reconciliation processes among themselves. There are signs of some theological convergence between opposed mission movements in recent years. And churches themselves have made significant progress towards shared baptism, eucharist and ministry and also toward common witness. We hope that these will lead to renewed relationships. The gospel of reconciliation is shared with integrity if the church is a reconciled and healing community.

68. If the goal and process of mission is to be reconciliation, it is imperative that the church revisit its past and engages in some introspection and self-examination about its *mission* in the world. Any credible mission by the church has to begin with the confession that not all of her mission has been a reflection of the mission which God has intended and which Godself carries out (*missio Dei*). If we have declared the love of God while hating our brother or sister, we are liars (1 John 4:20). Where Christian missionary enterprise was - and still is - complicit in an imperialistic project involving violence, causing destruction of indigenous cultures, fragmentation of communities and even division among Christians, it calls for repentance (metanoia). Repentance requires the confession of the sin of violent colonization in the name of the gospel. This is important for the "healing of memories", which is an integral part of the mission of reconciliation and healing. The church must take care to dress the wounds of the past (cf. Jer. 6:14f.).

69. While we confess these sins, we also acknowledge the fact that there has been, and is, much genuine Christian mission in the spirit of peace and reconciliation. Such mission results in peace with God, healed lives, restored communities and the socio-economic liberation of marginalized peoples.

Spirituality of reconciliation

70. Mission in terms of reconciliation and healing calls for a corresponding spirituality: one that is healing, transforming, liberating, and builds relationships of mutual respect. A genuine spirituality for reconciliation and healing reflects the interaction of faith and praxis that constitutes witness (*martyria*). Witness presupposes a spirituality of self-examination and confession of sins (*metanoia*), leading to proclamation (*kerygma*) of the gospel of reconciliation, service (*diakonia*) in love, worship (*leiturgia*) in truth, and teaching of justice. The exercise of these spiritual gifts builds up reconciled communities (*koinonia*).[17]

71. The spirituality of reconciliation is one of humility and self-emptying (kenosis; Phil. 2:7), and at the same time an experience of the Holy Spirit's sanctifying and transforming power. In his struggle to reconcile Jews and Gentiles and other factions, the apostle Paul declared that God's power is made perfect in weakness (2 Cor. 12:9; 1 Cor. 2:3-5). The spirituality of reconciliation is the spirituality of passion, resurrection as well as of Pentecost. In the global context of the return of imperialism - especially in the form of the hegemonic power of globalization - this self-emptying spirituality is a challenge both to the victims and perpetrators of systemic violence and injustice. The treasure we have is "in earthen vessels, to show that the transcendent power belongs to God and not to us" (2 Cor. 4:7). The church's mission in this context is once again to be in the "in-between-ness" - between the wielders of power and the powerless - to empower the powerless and also challenge the powerful to empty themselves of their power and privileges for the sake of the dis-empowered. The spirituality of reconciliation challenges the power structures of local communities, including the churches, in particular where traditional majority or folk churches act in a hegemonious way.

72. A self-emptying spirituality is also a spirituality of cross-bearing. The church is called to bear the cross of Jesus Christ, by being with the suffering.[18] A spirituality of non-violent resistance is an integral aspect of reconciliation and healing in an age of continuing exploitation of the poor and the marginalized. In situations of oppression, discrimination and hurt, the cross of Christ is the power of God for salvation (1 Cor. 1:18).

73. The sacraments and liturgical life of the church should express the mission of reconciliation and healing. Baptism is an act of sharing in the death and resurrection of Jesus Christ. It is symbolic of the spirituality of cross-bearing, which is both a dying to self (Mark 8:34 and parallels) and a raising up to life (John 3:14, etc.). The eucharist is a sacramental act of healing, an act of remembrance, and a re-enactment of the breaking of

the body of Christ for the sake of cosmic reconciliation. The bread of God, which comes down from heaven, gives life to the world (John 6:33). The sharing out of the bread and the wine among all calls for redistribution of wealth and the equality of the kingdom that Jesus Christ proclaimed. In prayer, the church intercedes with God for the world, standing in the "in-between-ness" in faith that God will bring reconciliation and healing. In preaching the word, the church brings comfort to the downtrodden, proclaims truth and justice, and calls all to repentance and forgiveness. The church's worship is itself a witness to the world of reconciliation in Christ, and in the power of the Spirit the church lives out this eucharistic witness in daily life.

74. Spiritual resources for reconciliation and healing are not confined to Christian faith traditions. This challenges us to take the interfaith dimensions of mission seriously, for reconciliation and healing in the holistic sense cannot be achieved without reconciliation amongst various faiths and cultures. One way of doing this is to appreciate and learn from the spiritual resources available in other faiths and cultures. Other traditions and experiences of healing and reconciliation, including those of Indigenous communities, are of great value.

75. The recent ecumenical statement on dialogue reminds us that "inter-religious dialogue is not an instrument to resolve problems instantly in emergency situations".[19] However, in times of conflict the relationships built up by patient dialogue during peacetime may prevent religion from being used as a weapon and, in many cases, pave the way for mediation and reconciliation initiatives. Dialogue presupposes mutual recognition, it signifies a willingness to reconcile and desire to live together. A process of dialogue can build up trust and allow for mutual witness, in this way it may be a means of healing. However, while dialogue is important, issues of truth, memory, repentance, justice, forgiveness and love may need to be addressed before dialogue is possible. The "in-betweenness" of the missionary praxis means that in some situations what is called for is the prophetic power of the

gospel to critique religious practices and beliefs that promote injustice and to bring about repentance.

76. The ministry of the Holy Spirit - in which the church is privileged to share - is to heal and reconcile a broken world. In order to exercise this mission with integrity, the church must be a community that is experiencing healing and reconciliation in Christ. The spirituality of reconciliation is self-emptying and cross-bearing in order that the saving power of God may be demonstrated. The Holy Spirit endows the church with gifts and resources for this ministry and, in the spirit of dialogue, Christians are open to appreciate the resources that people of other faiths bring to it. The mission of the church involves going between the parties that are estranged or in conflict. This means accompanying them in their struggles and at the same time challenging the powers of injustice and violence to bring about reconciliation. The goal is to build up reconciled and healing communities which are again missional in commitment and practical ministry.

5. Equipping for reconciliation: pedagogy, pastoralia and vision

77. In the mission of reconciliation we are inspired by the gospel vision of peace on earth (Luke 2:14). In his preaching of the kingdom of God in both word and deed, our lord Jesus Christ showed us what the kingdom of God is like. It is the kingdom of truth and justice, repentance and forgiveness, in which the first are last and the leaders are servants of all. In the epistles, the apostles taught the churches how to be communities of reconciliation. These bring forth the fruit of the Spirit: love, joy, peace, patience, kindness, goodness, faithfulness, gentleness and self-control (Gal. 5:22-23). Members are called to love one another, live at peace with one another, and bless those who persecute them, leaving vengeance to God (Rom. 12:9-21).

78. However, many have proclaimed peace where there is no peace and only superficially treated the deep wounds caused by broken relationships and injustice (Jer. 6:14). Any pedagogical

and pastoral approach to mission has to acknowledge the fact that the ministry of healing and reconciliation is a profound and often lengthy process that therefore requires long-term strategies (Rom. 8:25). Once the church believes that mission belongs to God, and that it is not a frenzied activity initiated by the church, then the church's mission will be oriented towards the long-term goal of creating communities of reconciliation and healing. The realization of our hope requires patience, pastoral sensitivity and an appropriate educational method.

79. Our sense of being human is key to this educational process. Human beings are essentially relational beings, linked together and active in the web of life. For our survival, we depend on one another and therefore we need to live in just relationships of trust and build communities of reconciliation and healing. From a Christian anthropological perspective, human beings are also forgiven beings, forgiven by God. Forgiveness as a theological category has ethical ramifications. The ministry of reconciliation and healing through forgiveness involves truth-telling and justice. In other words, the pedagogy of justice is what makes forgiveness a radical concept. Forgiveness that undermines justice is not Christian forgiveness. Costly discipleship, which is integral to the ministry of healing and reconciliation, has to be justice-oriented.

80. Compassion for the broken and concern for life in all its fullness are the pastoral modes of Christian mission. One of the most important sources for learning about this ministry is the immense wealth of people's day-to-day life experience, especially that of the poor and the vulnerable. The church's involvement in people's life experiences, in their struggles to affirm life wherever it is denied, is perhaps the best learning process. Through this pedagogy of shared memories, the church will be enabled to carry out its mission effectively.

81. Whereas the emphasis is being put in this document on social reconciliation processes, insights can be drawn for renewing and strengthening the pastoral approach to conflicts between

individual persons in family, work place and church. Reconciliation between persons also needs to address questions of truth, healing of memories, repentance, justice, forgiveness and love. Pastors, priests as well as lay members of the community have the most important and difficult task to find ways to journey with persons who suffer from deep wounds left by the hardship of life or interpersonal conflicts, to offer them a safe space for expressing their vulnerability, anger, helplessness, suffering and yearning. At personal level, too, to follow Christ's call to reconciliation may entail a long journey or process, needing time and the capacity to cope with success and failures, moments of hope and of despair, putting faith to the test. Not all churches have kept the tradition of the sacrament of confession and reconciliation, but all are encouraged to find a way to envisage their pastoral ministry in terms of the understanding of mission described in this document.

82. This pastoral healing ministry must be embedded in a community life where people find a home and a safe space in which joys and pains can be shared openly, where those feeling vulnerable find enough security to express what burdens them, a community in which love overcomes fear and judgment. Such communities, nourished by the celebration of the eucharist, become then as such missionary entities, because the gospel which is preached is also lived and experienced. That such communities also have a role to play in society and be welcoming even to those who are not regular members was forcefully described by Paul in Romans 12. That passage also reminds us that a reconciling and healing mission may lead to suffer persecution. Since Christ, many missionary persons and communities have also been victims of violence and discrimination. But even in such cases, the commandment to love is to be the overarching characteristic of Christian witness to God's reconciliation.

83. Equipping for mission in a paradigm of reconciliation has significant implications for existing models of theological and mission education and training. Imbuing the church with a ped-

agogy of justice and a compassionate pastoral theology brings challenges for both the content and the mode of instruction. As Christians engaging in a ministry of reconciliation we will continue to require the knowledge of language, culture and religious traditions that will help us enter into the experience of others and serve them. Equally importantly, we will need a theology and spirituality of reconciliation. We should together develop a theological understanding of how God effects reconciliation in the world and Christians' part in it. The church needs to learn and teach the dynamics and processes of reconciliation and the importance of the different dimensions of reconciliation ministry: establishing the truth, healing the memory, doing justice, receiving forgiveness and forgiving others. In order to overcome the contemporary culture of violence and counter the myth of redemptive violence, the church must demonstrate in its life and witness that justice and redemption is achieved through a nonviolent resistance. This requires a spirituality of reconciliation that is self-emptying and cross-bearing for the sake of justice. We also have a responsibility to use and develop the spiritual gifts that, used in the spirit of love, build up community and overcome disunity and enmity (1 Cor. 12:8-10, 13:1-3; see also Rom. 12:6-10).

84. The main theme of the 2005 conference on world mission and evangelism, "Come, Holy Spirit, heal and reconcile!", calls our attention to the mission of the Spirit. According to St John's gospel, the Holy Spirit who proceeds from the Father is the *parakletos*, who accompanies us in our brokenness. The Spirit, the intercessor, is in the "in-betweenness", going between the Father, the Son and all creation. The *parakletos* is the Spirit of truth who leads us into all truth and interprets to us the teaching of Jesus. The Holy Spirit unites us to God the Father and the Son and makes us part of the *missio Dei* to bring life to the world. The Spirit teaches us to abide in Christ and to love one another, thus witnessing to the love of Christ. In a situation of enmity, the Spirit comforts us and gives us courage to speak and declare the word of God. The *parakletos* consoles the suffering and con-

vinces the world of sin and righteousness and God's judgment. The Spirit, who is our counsellor, is the Spirit of peace in a violent world (John 14:15-16:15).

85. The *parakletos* provides a model and the medium for the church's ministry of reconciliation. The Holy Spirit heals and reconciles by coming alongside to inspire, enlighten and empower. In the Spirit, we are enabled to affirm what is true and at the same time to discern what is false and evil. The Spirit binds us together and in the Spirit we enjoy true communion and fellowship (2 Cor. 13:13). Though for a little while we, and all creation, groan like a woman in childbirth, the Spirit is our midwife and when the mission is accomplished we believe that our sorrow will turn to joy at the new life of reconciliation (John 16:20-22; Rom. 8:18-25).

The final vision

86. At the very end of the Bible, in the Book of Revelation, St John set down the vision given to him of the new heaven and new earth, the new creation that is the result of God's reconciling work in Christ (Rev. 21:1,5; cf. 2 Cor. 5:17-18). The New Jerusalem is the reconciled city where God dwells with God's people. In this city there is no longer any mourning or crying or pain because justice has been done; nor is there any darkness because everything is in the light of the glory of God. Through the centre of the city runs the river of life for the healing of the nations (Rev. 21:1-22:5). In the field of world mission we can, therefore, speak of the "oikoumene which is to come" (Heb. 2:5, cf. 13:14ff.), as an open society, where an honest dialogue between the existing living cultures can take place. The world today can and must become a *household (oikos)*, where everyone is open to the "other" (as they are open to the Ultimate Other, i.e. God), and where all can share a common life, despite the plurality and difference of their identity. Reconciliation as a new mission paradigm results in a new understanding of the term oikoumene and its derivatives (ecumenism etc.). These terms no longer exclusively refer to an abstract universality,

such as the entire inhabited world, or the whole human race, or even a united universal church. In other words they no longer describe a given situation, but substantial - and at the same time threatened - relations between churches, between cultures, between people and human societies, and at the same time between humanity and the rest of God's creation.

6. Questions for further study and discussion

87. This attempt towards a theology of mission as reconciliation raises a number of questions that will need further and more detailed attention. These include:

- What are the practical implications of the call for economic reconciliation?

- "What are the processes that can bring Muslim-Christian reconciliation in the present context?

- "What contributions does Pentecostal and charismatic thinking and experience make to mission theology of reconciliation?

- "In what ways can the theology of the Holy Spirit (pneumatology) further aid the practice of and reflection on reconciliation?

- "How does a renewed focus on pneumatology transform humankind's relation with creation?

- "What changes does mission as reconciliation suggest to existing paradigms of mission? In particular, what does it mean for the understanding of conversion?

- "How can the importance of the spirit of reconciliation in mission be effectively communicated to those using aggressive missionary methods?

- "How can we resource and develop appropriate ways to equip local churches to become reconciling and healing communities?

- "How can the churches support those specially called and gifted in the ministry of reconciliation?

1 *Mission and Evangelism: An Ecumenical Affirmation,* WCC, 1982, approved by the central committee of the WCC.
2 *Mission and Evangelism in Unity Today,* CWME conference preparatory paper no 1. Statement adopted as a study document by the CWME Commission in the year 2000.
3 During the Salvador conference, a particularly important and moving celebration took place at the Solar do Unhão dock , the place where the ships loaded with slaves and coming from Africa landed. Representatives from both European and African origin expressed repentance from participation in the sin of slavery and asked for forgiveness. Cf. Jean S. Stromberg, "From Each Culture, with One Voice. Worship at Salvador", in Christopher Duraisingh ed., *Called to One Hope: The Gospel in Diverse Cultures,* WCC, 1998, pp.166-76.
4 *Called to One Hope,* pp.27 and 28. Acts of commitment of the 1996 world mission conference in Salvador da Bahía, Brazil.
5 *Mission and Evangelism in Unity Today,* §39.
6 *Ibid.,* §13.
7 WCC Unit II, Churches in Mission: Education, Health, Witness: *Preparatory Papers for Section Work, Conference on World Mission and Evangelism,* Salvador da Bahía, WCC, 1996, p.19. *Mission and Evangelism in Unity Today,* §62.
8 As in South Africa.
9 As in Guatemala.
10 The murder of Bishop Gerardi in Guatemala after he announced the results of such a report is a chilling reminder of this.
11 As for example the "mothers of the disappeared" in Argentina.
12 *Mission and Evangelism in Unity Today,* §13.
13 *Ibid.,* §§ 9 and 13.
14 *Ibid.,* §14.
15 Reference to John V.Taylor *The Go-Between God: the Holy Spirit and Christian Mission,* London, SCM, 1972.
16 *"The Challenge of Proselytism and the Calling to Common Witness", appendix C of the Seventh Report of the Joint Working Group between the Roman Catholic Church and the World Council of Churches,* Geneva-Rome 1998, p.45, §§8 and 9.
17 *Mission and Evangelism in Unity Today,* §7.
18 For example, the Ecumenical Accompaniment Programme in Palestine and Israel aims to be with Palestinians and Israelis in their non-violent actions and concerted advocacy efforts to end the occupation.
19 *Ecumenical Considerations for Dialogue and Relations with People of Other Religions: Taking Stock of 30 Years of Dialogue and Revisiting the 1979 Guidelines,* WCC, 2003, §28.

The Healing Mission of the Church

Presentation

This document was prepared at a meeting held in Geneva in December 2004 by a group of 12 missiologists, medical doctors and health professionals, together with WCC staff. The document was finalized and published on the website of the Athens world mission conference in January 2005 as conference preparatory paper no. 11. The first paragraph sets out the intention of the paper and how it relates to earlier WCC documents. The Commission on World Mission and Evangelism approved the plan to publish such a document and several commissioners were part of the drafting committee. However, the document has not been presented to the Commission nor to any governing body of the WCC prior to its publication in this book. It is to be read in conjunction with the paper on "mission as ministry of reconciliation" as a major input to the world mission conference in Athens, May 2005, and to discussion of the conference theme "Come, Holy Spirit, Heal and Reconcile! Called in Christ to be Healing and Reconciling Communities".

The paper closely connects experiences and reflections of the WCC and its former Christian Medical Commission (CMC) on a holistic approach to the healing ministry with recent developments in ecumenical missiology. It shows the fruits that can be gained by reclaiming the link existing in the New Testament between healing, witness and the church. Whereas there had been a connection between healing and mission in the 1960s when the CMC was created,[1] it was only in the years following the Harare assembly in 1998 that an intentional merger of both traditions and networks was advocated within the WCC, leading to the formation of a new staff team, the formulation of the theme of the world mission conference in Athens, and the study process reflected in this paper. These moves may be considered an important development in ecumenical mission history.

Some chapters of the paper explore new avenues for ecumenical missiology, in particular by opening the debate on healing and world-views,[2] including the relation of healing to the concept of spiritual powers. It focuses intentionally on the importance of the spiritual life of the local community as an asset in its capacity to be a healing community. For that, the authors of the paper draw on the ancient liturgical traditions of Anglican, Orthodox and Roman Catholic churches. The healing ministry is set in the context of a trinitarian understanding of missio Dei, and controversial questions are faced, such as the relation between illness and sin or how to discern what healing may mean if experienced in the context of other religious traditions. The paper does not emphasize elements of the healing ministry recently dealt with in WCC statements[3] but focuses on other theological and practical questions which seem important challenges and opportunities for churches wanting to respond positively to the desire for healing in contemporary contexts. There is an intentional effort at pursuing an incipient dialogue with Christians coming from the charismatic movement and Pentecostal churches.[4] It was the conviction of the drafters of the paper that many Christians and churches can be enriched by sharing their perception of the manifold ways in which God is healing today, through spiritual, medical or other means.

JM

1 The Christian Medical Commission (CMC) was established by the central committee of the WCC in 1967 following two consultations held in Tübingen, at the German Institute for Medical Missions, in 1964 and 1967. During the first years of its existence, the CMC was linked to the then Division of World Mission and Evangelism of the WCC. Later the CMC became associated with the Programme Unit on Justice and Service. Cf. Christoph Benn and Erlinda Senturias, "Health, Healing and Wholeness in the Ecumenical Discussion", *IRM*, vol. 90, nos 356/357, Jan.-April 2001, pp.7-25. That whole double issue on "Health, Faith and Healing" carries the documents on an important consultation held in Hamburg, Germany, which launched the most recent study process on the healing ministry and mission.

2 Which is a late follow-up of the emphasis of the world mission conference in Salvador, Brazil, on the relation between the gospel and cultures.

3 In 1996, the central committee adopted a statement entitled "The Impact of HIV/AIDS and the Churches' Response", published in *Facing AIDS: The Challenge, the Churches' Response: A WCC Study Document*, WCC, 1997, pp.96-108.

4 Documents and provisional results of the dialogue with Pentecostals are published in IRM, vol. 93, nos 370-371, July -Oct. 2004, "Divine Healing, Pentecostalism and Mission".

The Healing Mission of the Church

Introductory remarks

1. The present document has been prepared by a multicultural and interdenominational group of missiologists, medical doctors and health professionals. It builds upon the tradition of the WCC's Christian Medical Commission (CMC) and its most fruitful contribution to an understanding of the healing ministry of the church. This document does not repeat what remains well formulated in earlier texts of the World Council of Churches, such as the document "Healing and Wholeness: The Churches' Role in Health", adopted in 1990 by the central committee. That text situates the healing ministry within the struggle for justice, peace and the integrity of creation, and remains an essential contribution, the urgency of which has even grown in a now globalized world. The present study document concentrates mainly on some medical and theological-spiritual aspects of the healing ministry and their link with a recent ecumenical understanding of mission. It is offered as a background document to the 2005 Athens conference on world mission and evangelism and an important contribution to a dialogue on the relevance of its theme:

Come, Holy Spirit, heal and reconcile!
Called in Christ to be reconciling and healing communities

It is to be read together with the study document recommended by the Commission on World Mission and Evangelism on "mission as ministry of reconciliation".[1] The present document does not pretend to make any final statement on healing or mission, but hopes to enrich the debate and enable Christians and churches to better respond to their calling.

1. The context

The global context of health and disease at the beginning of the 21st century

2. Global statistics on the incidence and prevalence of diseases, on the burden of diseases for communities and societies, and on mortality rates, are based on a scientific concept of disease and epidemiological methods for measuring disease and its impact.[2] In medical science, disease refers to identifiable dysfunction of human physiology. We have to acknowledge that this approach is inherently different from a more holistic interpretation of health and diseases used in WCC circles[3] and that is not quantifiable with current methods and therefore not easily suitable for statistical analyses.

3. It may anyhow be misleading to describe a global context because the situation is extremely complex and varies enormously between continents and societies, and increasingly also within societies and even within local communities, depending on economic resources which influence living conditions, lifestyle behaviour and access to health care. Any overview will be grossly misleading if taken as an accurate description of local or regional situations.

4. Nevertheless some trends can be discerned. One can speak of a worldwide improvement in health if measured in terms of premature mortality and disability adjusted life years, except for those regions heavily affected by HIV/AIDS. Infant mortality which is a sensitive indicator for general living conditions and access to basic health care has reached very low levels in Europe and North America and is going down particularly in East and South-east Asia as well as Latin America and the Caribbean. It is still very high or even increasing in a number of countries in sub-Saharan Africa.

5. Other major trends include the *global increase in chronic disease*, particularly mental diseases and diseases affecting the elder-

ly. Even in low-income countries there is an increasing number of adults suffering e.g. from coronary heart disease, cancer or diabetes which are the most common causes of morbidity and mortality in industrialized countries.[4] What is most disturbing is the general trend for a long-term increase in the number of people suffering from psychiatric diseases, particularly depression, both in countries of the North and the South. Accelerated and aggravated experiences of crisis and threat following rapid globalization processes seem to put excessive pressure on the human psychic system.

6. Currently the international community is engaged in a major review of the global health status as part of the process to assess progress towards the achievement of the Millennium Development Goals (MDG). Three of the eight MDGs are directly referring to health.[5]

7. The impact of *human-made climate change* and deterioration of the natural environment on the global health situation cannot yet be sufficiently mapped and measured, but raises serious concerns as to its potential devastating effects, not only locally, but worldwide. Deforestation e.g. contributes to building up the greenhouse gases in the atmosphere which results in the depletion of the stratospheric ozone and increases ultra-violet radiation. This induces the suppression of immune systems and permit the emergence of cancers and certain infectious diseases that depend on cell mediated immune responses. Global warming leading to a rise of the surface water levels of oceans occasions the flooding of human dwelling places thereby increasing the incident of waterborne diseases. Global warming also leads to the resurgence of malaria and other infectious diseases in temperate countries and increases the danger of cardiovascular illnesses.

8. Despite the advanced technology, the *health state of the world* is still preoccupying as shown in the 2004 World Health Organization report.[6]

It has therefore be pointed out that health and healing are not just medical issues. They embrace political, social, economical, cultural and spiritual dimensions. As it is stated in the WCC document "Healing and Wholeness: The Churches' Role in Health":
"... although the 'health industry' is producing and using progressively sophisticated and expensive technology, the increasingly obvious fact is that most of the world's health problems cannot be best addressed in this way... It is an acknowledged fact that the number one cause of disease in the world is poverty, which is ultimately the result of oppression, exploitation and war. Providing immunizations, medicines, and even health education by standard methods cannot significantly ameliorate illness due to poverty..." [7]

Unequal access to health services - health and justice as ethical challenges

9. The fact remains that in large parts of the world people have no access to essential health services. The question of affordable *access to health care provisions* and the commercialization of health constitute yet other very complex and sensitive issues.

In the one hand scientifically based health care becomes ever more expensive with increased levels of diagnostic and therapeutic sophistication widening the gap between those who can afford it and those who cannot. This gets most pronounced in low-income countries but becomes increasingly visible also in high-income countries with reduced public expenditure on health. Christians have to be constantly reminded that access to health care is an essential human right and not a commodity that should be available only for those with sufficient financial resources.

10. On the other hand there is an increased interest in addressing diseases of poverty, in particular the major infectious diseases HIV/AIDS, tuberculosis and malaria. The creation of the Global Fund to Fight AIDS, Tuberculosis and Malaria by the United Nations is a case in point. Christians have advocated

strongly for increased attention to and financial resources for diseases of poverty to achieve greater equity in the distribution of resources. Several global campaigns or initiatives testify to this concern, such as the Ecumenical Advocacy Alliance and the Ecumenical HIV/AIDS Initiative in Africa. On such global health questions, there are also increasing efforts at cooperation between various faith-based communities.

11. Even if in some instances, good health-care services help to alleviate poverty, health and healing cannot be disconnected from structural organization of our societies, the quality of relationship among people and the life-style.

Increasingly widespread unhealthy life-style patterns[8] are a consequence of standards and interests of the food industry and of changing cultural behaviours promoted among others by media and the advertisement industry.

12. The present state could be summarized in terms such as:

Today, in our globalized and highly commercial world, people are far from being all healthy, neither as individuals nor as communities, and this despite the many advances in preventive medicine and therapeutic skills.

- Many people do not have access to affordable medical care.

- While preventable diseases are still a major problem in many parts of the world, chronic illnesses often related to life-style and behaviour are on the rise, causing much suffering all over the world.

- A growing number of people with mental illnesses are being recognized today.

- The costs of medical care have risen to prohibitive levels, making the technology unavailable to many and leading to medical systems becoming unsustainable.

- High technology has an inhuman face, leading to people feeling isolated and fragmented.

- Death in modern medicine is seen as failure and is aggressively fought to such an extent that people are not able to die with dignity.

13. People disenchanted with the established medical system are looking for more than treatment of a sick liver or heart. They want to be seen and treated as persons. Their diseases often lead them to ask spiritual questions and there is a growing search for the spiritual dimension of healing.

The importance of the role of the community in creating and maintaining health is being rediscovered in many of the affluent countries.

14. Scientific researchers have started to map what they call the "religious health assets" in order to provide basic data on potential material infrastructure and spiritual contributions by religious communities to national and international health policy.

A number of epidemiological studies carried out by medical professionals, mainly in the USA, highlighting the positive effect of religion and spirituality on health are enabling a new dialogue between the medical and theological disciplines.[9] Scientific medicine itself has become increasingly interested in the spiritual dimension of the human person.

Healing and culture: different world-views, cultural conditions and their impact on understanding health and healing

15. The way health and healing are defined, sickness and illness explained, depends largely on culture and conventions. In ecumenical mission circles, culture is usually understood in a wide sense, including not only literature, music and arts, but values, structures, world-view, ethics, as well as religion.[10]

16. It is in particular the combination of religion, world-view and values that impacts people's specific understanding of and

approach to healing. Since culture varies from continent to continent and from country to country or even within countries and groups of people, there is no immediate universal common understanding of the main causes of sickness and illness or of any evil affecting humans.

17. There are cultures in which supernatural beings are seen as the real ultimate causative agents for ill health, particularly mental disorders. In such world-views, people go to traditional healers and religious specialists for exorcism and deliverance from evil spirits and demons. Only then can they have the guarantee that the ultimate cause of their suffering has been dealt with. This would not exclude parallel treatments of symptoms with herbs, traditional or industrially manufactured drugs.

18. Masses of people integrate popular religious beliefs and culture in their understanding of health and healing. We may call this popular religiosity and belief in health. This belief may involve veneration of saints, pilgrimages to shrines, and use of religious symbols such as oil and amulets to protect people from evil spirits or evil intentions that harm people.

19. Others, in particular Asian cultures, also point to the importance of harmony within the human body as the necessary precondition for a person's health, well-being and healing. Shibashi, e.g., an ancient Chinese practice of nature-oriented movements attune the body to the rhythm of nature producing an energizing effect. The traditional belief is that healing and health are actual effects of balance in the flow of energy that are affected from within and outside the human body. The clogging of centres of energy (chakras) or obstruction in the flow of energy causes illness. Acupuncture or finger pressure are other modalities of balancing the flow of energy.

20. Out of different world-views culture-specific medical sciences and systems developed in some of the major civilizations of the world. In particular since the Enlightenment, these were disregarded by the Western medical establishment, but are now

again increasingly considered worthy alternatives for the treatment of specific illnesses.

21. As a result of advances in medical science and of intercultural exchanges, some people, in particular in Western contexts, develop new life-styles emphasizing walking, jogging, aerobic exercise, healthy diet, yoga and other forms of meditation, massage and going to sauna and spa as a way to achieve wellness, health and healing. These may well bring relief from stressful situations and some chronic illnesses like cardiovascular diseases and diabetes mellitus.

22. Certain forms of nature-centred religiosity and indigenous and emerging secular cultures also point to the relationship between cosmology or ecology and health and healing. There is a growing, however still insufficient awareness of the importance of linking ecology and health. The determinants of health are clean water and air and a safe space for all living creatures. Deforestation has profoundly damaged the water supply, polluted the air, and destroyed the habitats of many living creatures, turning them into "pests" and creating ill health among human beings and other elements of creation. Very close associations of animals and human beings are now the cause of new forms of epidemics such as the emergence of avian flu, a severe and potentially fatal viral infection that is transferred from ducks and chickens to human beings. The tsunami event and post-tsunami situation highlights the importance of taking care not only of human beings but of the whole of creation and of attuning oneself to the rhythm of nature.

2. Health and Healing and the Ecumenical Movement

23. In ancient times, the art of healing belonged to priests. They were consulted in the case of disease and often were regarded as mediators of healing. The unity of body, mind and spirit was understood and accepted.

The centrality of healing in the mission of the early church

24. It is worth recalling that the growth of the early church in the 2nd and 3rd century was - among other factors - also due to the fact that Christianity presented itself as a healing movement to the early Mediterranean societies. The importance of the different healing ministries within the church is reflected by the early accounts of mission in the New Testament. Many writings of the early church fathers also affirm the centrality of the church as a healing community and proclaim Christ as the healer of the world over against Hellenistic religiosity.

25. In affirming that God himself in the life of his Son has lived through experiences of weakness unto even experiencing death himself, Christianity revolutionized the understanding of God and profoundly transformed the basic attitudes of the faith community to the sick, the aged and the dying. It contributed decisively to break up the conventional strategies and mechanisms of exclusion, of discrimination and of religious stigmatization of the sick and the fragile. It put an end to the association of the divine with ideals of a perfect, sane, beautiful and un-passionate existence. The different attitude to the sick, to the widows and to the poor proved to be a vital source for the missionary success and vitality of the early church. The monasteries continued to be islands of hope by caring for the sick.

Medical science and medical missions

26. Over the centuries the development of science and technology, and especially since the Enlightenment, have led to a change in the understanding of the human being and of health. Instead of being regarded as an indivisible unity, the human being was fragmented into body, mind and soul. Medical professionals tend to view a disease as a malfunction of a wonderful and complicated machine to be repaired with the help of medical skills, neglecting the fact that human beings have a soul and a mind. The rise of the disciplines of psychology and psychiatry accentuated this divide taking over the care of the mind. As a result, there was loss of the

understanding of the concept of wholeness, as well as of the role of the community and of spirituality in health.

27. Medical missions came about some time later, i.e. in the 19th century, leading to the setting up of church-related health-care systems in many parts of the world where missionaries were active. Health care was seen by some as an essential part of the mission of the sending church or missionary organization. Though these mission hospitals provided compassionate care of high quality at low cost, the Western medical model of health care was often superimposed on indigenous local cultures with their own therapeutic and healing traditions. However, many medical missionaries engaged in training indigenous people in the art of healing and nursing from the very start of their medical mission.

A holistic and balanced understanding of the Christian ministry of healing

28. A carefully designed, most comprehensive study process initiated by the World Council of Churches' Christian Medical Commission (CMC) in the 1970s and 1980s showed that many factors or influences are responsible for forms of illness and broken relationships, and growing feelings of void and lack of spiritual orientation in people's lives; weaken the natural defences of the body to cope or defend oneself from infections or bio-chemical disturbances in bodily functions or other forms of physical, emotional, or mental disorders; cause imbalance in the flow of energy leading to obstruction and manifestation of dis-ease; provoke enslavement or addiction from evil desires or influences that hinder the person's response to God's saving grace.

29. According to an anthropology rooted in the biblical-theological tradition of the church, the human being is seen as "multidimensional unity".[11] Body, soul and mind are not separate entities, but inter-related and inter-dependent. Therefore, health has physical, psychological and spiritual dimensions. The individual being is also part of the community; health has also a social dimension. And because of the interaction between the natural

environment (biosphere) and persons or communities, health has even an ecological dimension.

30. This has led the World Council of Churches to offer the following **definition of health**:

Health is a dynamic state of well-being of the individual and society, of physical, mental, spiritual, economic, political, and social well-being - of being in harmony with each other, with the material environment and with God.[12]

Such a holistic view underlines that health is not a static concept in which clear distinction lines are drawn between those who are healthy and those who are not. Every human being is constantly moving between different degrees of staying healthy and of struggling with infections and diseases. Such an understanding of health is close to the one emerging in the more recent debate and research on health promoting factors.[13]

Such a holistic view has also consequences on the understanding of the church's mission:

The Christian ministry of healing includes both the practice of medicine (addressing both physical and mental health) as well as caring and counselling disciplines and spiritual practices. Repentance, prayer and/or laying-on of hands, divine healing, rituals involving touch and tenderness, forgiveness and the sharing of the eucharist can have important and at times even dramatic effects in the physical as well as social realm of human beings. All the different means are part of God's work in creation and presence in the church. Contemporary scientific medicine as well as other medical approaches make use of what is available in the world God has created. Healing through "medical means" is not to be thought of as inferior (or even unnecessary) to healing through other or by "spiritual" means.

31. There are churches and social contexts (particularly in Western post-Enlightenment and modern societies) in which a one-sided emphasis and attention was given to the achievements

of contemporary scientific medicine and the physical aspects of health and healing. Here a new openness and attention is needed for the spiritual dimensions in the Christian ministries of healing. There are other contexts and churches in which - due to a different world-view and the non-availability of modern Western medical systems - the importance of spiritual healing is highly valued. Here also a new dialogue between spiritual healing practices and approaches in modern medicine is essential.

Recent attempts to deepen the understanding of the healing mission of the church

32. One of the most thorough recent studies was conducted on behalf of the Church of England by a working party commissioned by the House of Bishops. It produced a remarkably encompassing report developing a definition of healing as a "process towards health and wholeness... It embraces what God has achieved for human beings through the incarnation of Jesus Christ... God's gifts of healing are occasionally experienced instantly or rapidly but in most cases healing is a gradual process taking time to bring deep restoration to health at more than one level."[14]

33. It is both significant that at the beginning of the 21st century several important ecumenical church meetings such as the Lutheran World Federation's (LWF) assembly in Winnipeg, Canada, the assembly of the Conference of European Churches (CEC) in Trondheim, Norway, the general council of the World Alliance of Reformed Churches (WARC) in Accra, Ghana, have focused directly or indirectly on the healing ministry of the church in a world torn by suffering and violence. The following extract from the most recent mission document of the LWF shall stand for many of those efforts:

"According to the scriptures, God is the source of all healing. In the Old Testament, healing and salvation are inter-related and in many instances mean the same thing: 'Heal me, o Lord, and I shall be healed; save me, and I shall be saved' (Jer. 17:14). The

New Testament, however, does not equate being cured from an ailment with being saved. The New Testament also makes a distinction between curing and healing. Some may be cured but not healed (Luke 17:15-19), while others are not cured but healed (2 Cor. 12:7-9). 'Cure' denotes restoring lost health and thus carries a protological view. Healing refers to the eschatological reality of abundant life that breaks in through the event of Jesus Christ, the wounded healer, who participates in all aspects of human suffering, dying, and living, and overcomes violation, suffering, and death by his resurrection. In this sense, healing and salvation point to the same eschatological reality."[15]

Recent dialogue of world-views re. the reality of spiritual powers

34. In recent years, largely because of the rapid growth of Pentecostal-charismatic movements and their influence across the ecumenical spectrum, terms such as "power encounter", "demon[ology]", and "principalities and powers", have become topics of missiological interest and research today as has the question of divine healing in particular. Exorcism, casting out evil spirits, and "witch-demonology" are also terms more frequently used in certain Christian circles today.[16]

Talk about demons and evil spirits is, of course, not a new phenomenon either in Christian theology nor church life. The Christian church, throughout her history - especially during the first centuries and later, more often among enthusiastic, charismatic renewal movements - has either appointed specially gifted/graced persons to tackle evil forces (exorcists) or at least acknowledged the reality of spiritual powers.

35. The rapid proliferation of Christian churches among the cultures outside of the West, has also contributed to the rise to prominence of the theme of demonology. Christians in Africa, Asia, Latin America and the Pacific tend to be much more open to the idea of the reality of these forces. In many of those cultures, there is a widespread involvement with spiritual powers even apart from Christian faith..

One of the main reasons why the Western churches - especially the mainline Protestant churches - eschewed the whole topic of spiritual powers for several centuries has to do with the specific nature of their world-view going back to the influence of the Enlightenment. Christian theology and the way clergy was trained did not only ignore the topic but often also helped "demythologize" even the biblical talk about demons and spiritual powers. Earlier documents of WCC on healing and health have not tackled the issue adequately either.[17] Currently, a paradigm shift is taking place in Western culture - often referred to as "post-modernity"- which is challenging a narrow rationalistic world-view and theology.

3. Health and Healing in Biblical and Theological Perspective

God's healing mission

36. God Father, Son and Spirit leads creation and humanity towards the full realization of God's kingdom,which the prophets announce and expect as reconciled and healed relationships between creation and God, humanity and God, humanity and creation, between humans as persons and as groups or societies (healing in the fullest sense as "shalom", Isa. 65:17-25). This in missiology is referred to as missio Dei. In a trinitarian perspective, the creational, social-relational and spiritual-energetical dimensions of healing are interdependant, interwoven.

While affirming the dynamic reality of God's mission in world and creation, we also acknowledge its profound mystery which is beyond the grasp of human knowledge (Job 38f.). We rejoice whenever God's presence manifests itself in miraculous and liberating, healing, changes in human life and history, enabling life in dignity. We also cry out with the Psalmist and Job to challenge the Creator when evil and unexplainable suffering scandalize us and seem to indicate the absence of a merciful and just God: "Why, o God? Why me, Lord? How long?" It is in a profoundly ambivalent and paradoxical world that we affirm our belief and hope in a God who heals and cares.

37. As Christians, we acknowledge the perfect image of God as manifest in Jesus Christ, who came to witness through his life, deeds and words how God cares for humanity and creation. The incarnation of God in Christ affirms that God's healing power is not saving us from this world or above all material and bodily matters but is taking place in the midst of this world and all its pain, brokenness and fragmentation and that healing encompasses all of human existence.

Jesus Christ is the core and centre of God's mission, the personalization of God's kingdom. In the power of the Holy Spirit, Jesus of Nazareth was a healer, exorcist, teacher, prophet, guide and inspirator. He brought and offered freedom from sin, evil, suffering, illness, sickness, brokenness, hatred and disunity (Luke 4:16ff., Matt. 11:2-6). Hallmarks of the healings of Jesus Christ were his sensitivity to needs of people, especially the vulnerable, the fact that he was 'touched' and responded by healing (Luke 8:42b-48), his willingness to listen and openness to change (Mark 7:24b-30), his unwillingness to accept delay in alleviation of suffering (Luke 13:10-13) and his authority over traditions and evil spirits. Jesus' healings always brought about a complete restoration of body and mind unlike what we normally experience in healings.

38. He inaugurated the new creation, the "end of time" (*eschaton*) through signs and wonders which do point to the fullness of life, the abolition of suffering and death, promised by God as announced by the prophets. But these miraculous actions were not more than signs or signposts. Christ healed those who came or were brought to him. He did not however heal all the sick of his time. The kingdom of God, already present, is still expected. "Healing is a journey into perfection of the final hope, but this perfection is not always fully realised in the present (Rom. 8:22)."[18]

39. Jesus' healing and exorcist activity points in particular to the accomplishment of his ministry at the cross: he came to offer salvation, the healing of relationship with God, what Paul later described as "reconciliation" (2 Cor. 5). This he did through

service and sacrifice, fulfilling the ministry of the "wounded healer" prophesied by Isaiah (52:13-53:12). Christ's death on the cross is thus both protest against all suffering (Mark 15:34) and victory over sin and evil. By resurrecting Christ, God vindicated his ministry and gave it lasting significance. The cross and resurrection of Christ affirms that God's healing power is not staying apart and above the reality of pain, brokenness and dying but is reaching down to the very depth of human and creational suffering bringing light and hope in the uttermost depth of darkness and despair. The image of the resurrected Christ may be encountered among people who suffer (Matt. 25:31-46) as well as among vulnerable and wounded healers (Matt. 28:20, 10:16; 2 Cor. 12:9; John 15:20).

40. In ecumenical missiology, the Holy Spirit, Lord and life-giving, is believed to be active in church and world. The ongoing work of the Holy Spirit in the whole of creation initiating signs and foretastes of the new creation (2 Cor. 5:17) affirms that the healing power of God transcends all limits of places and times and is at work inside as well as outside the Christian church transforming humanity and creation in the perspective of the world to come.

God the Holy Spirit is the fountain of life for Christian individual and community life (John 7:37-39). The Spirit enables the church for mission and equips her with manifold charisms, including (e.g.) the one to heal (cure) by prayer and imposition of hands, the gift of consolation and pastoral care for those whose suffering seems without end, the charism of exorcism to cast out evil spirits, the authority of prophecy to denounce the structural sins responsible for injustice and death, and the charism of wisdom and knowledge essential to scientific research and the exercise of medical professions. But God the Holy Spirit also empowers the Christian community to forgive, share, heal wounds, overcome divisions and so journey towards full communion. The Spirit pursues thus, widens and universalises Christ's healing and reconciling mission.

Groaning in church and creation (Rom. 8), the Spirit also actualizes Christ's solidarity with the suffering and so witnesses to the power of God's grace that may also manifest itself paradoxically in weakness or illness (2 Cor. 12:9).

41. The Spirit fills the church with the transforming authority of the resurrected Lord who heals and liberates from evil, and with the compassion of the suffering Servant who dies for the world's sin and consoles the downtrodden. A Spirit-led healing mission encompasses both bold witness and humble presence.

Health, healing and the concept of spiritual powers

42. One of the dominant traits in which the healing ministry of Jesus is presented in the NT is that of ultimate authority over all life deforming and life destroying powers including death (Luke 7:11-17; John 11:11; Mark 5:35-43). Biblical world-view takes for granted the reality of the unseen world and attributes power and authority to spirits and the spiritual world.

43. In Jesus Christ the kingdom of God was at hand (Matt. 4:17, Luke 11:20) making demons "shudder" (James 2:19) because they realized that Christ had come to "destroy the works of the devil" (1 John 3:8; see Col. 2:15). Since numerous biblical healing narratives refer to demons and evil spirits as the cause of disease, exorcism becomes - consequently - one of the most common remedies (Mark 1:23-28, 5:9, 7:32-35; Luke 4:33-37; Matt. 8:16; John 5:1-8) for diagnosis rules therapy. There is thus indeed a form of healing which in the Bible is presented as a power encounter between Christ and the evil forces, a specific form of the healing mission particularly highlighted in several churches today, especially those with Pentecostal and charismatic background.

44. Through resurrection and ascension, Christ has overcome all evil powers. In the liturgy, the church celebrates this victory. Through its witness and mission, the church manifests that the powers - all the powers - have been defeated and so stripped of their binding influence on human lives. Those who follow Christ

dare in his name to denounce and challenge all other powers, thus bringing good news: "Go, preach, saying, the kingdom of heaven is at hand! Heal the sick, cleanse the lepers, raise the dead, cast out demons!" (Matt.10:7; cf. Mark 16:9-20).

45. This implies that the churches' ministry of proclaiming the gospel has to consciously address and name the powers, taking up the struggle with evil in whatever way it presents itself. These powers are not to be tampered with but recognized, because their reality rests in the hold they have over people who relate to them as the vital coordinates in life.

This issue of relationship between demonology/powers and healing needs careful study. How to interpret the reality and influence of powers in contemporary contexts and cultures is one of the urgent ecumenical debates.[19]

Illness, healing and sin: the "already and not yet" of the kingdom

46. Whereas in Christ evil and sin have been overcome, there are still many disasters, illnesses, deficiencies and diseases (physical, moral, spiritual and social) that seem to deny the arrival of the kingdom of God. The Bible knows the tradition saying that disease or disaster can be divine answer to sin, individual or collective. The prophets have repeatedly challenged God's people to repent from its disobedience to God's word. The New Testament knows of the potential relation between sin and sickness (1 Cor. 11:28-34). There is however a strong insistence by Jesus on denying any direct relationship between personal sin and sickness: "Who sinned? This man or his parents?... this is to manifest the power of God" (John 9:2). Similarly, in his answers to questions related to disasters, Jesus leaves open the question of their origin (Luke 13:1-5) and instead points to the urgency of turning back to God and follow the life he offers.

47. Suffering continues in the period between Easter and the end of history. The gospels do not explain this mystery. But the Spirit strengthens the church for its healing and reconciling mis-

sion and enables people to cope with continuing suffering and illness in the light of Christ's redemption. Because Christ has paid the price for all sin and brings salvation, no power has final damaging influence on those who put their confidence in God's love manifested in Christ (Rom. 8:31-39).

48. In the end, Christ will hand over the kingdom to his Father (1 Cor. 15:24), free of illness, suffering and death. In this kingdom healing will be complete. There is found the common root of healing and salvation (*salus*). "He will wipe every tear from their eyes. Death will be no more: mourning and crying and pain will be no more" (Rev. 21:4).

4. The Church as a Healing Community

Church, community and mission

49. The nature and mission of the church proceeds from the triune God's own identity and mission with its emphasis on community in which there is sharing in a dynamics of interdependence. It belongs to the very essence of the church - understood as the body of Christ created by the Holy Spirit - to live as a healing community, to recognize and nurture healing charisms and to maintain ministries of healing as visible signs of the presence of the kingdom of God.[20]

50. To be a reconciling and healing community is an essential expression of the mission of the church to create and renew relationships in the perspective of the kingdom of God. This means to proclaim Christ's grace and forgiveness, to heal bodies, minds, souls and to reconcile broken communities in the perspective of fullness of life (John 10:10).

51. It has to be reaffirmed what the document "Mission and Evangelism in Unity Today"[21] stated, i.e. that "mission carries a holistic understanding: the proclamation and sharing of the good news of the gospel, by word (*kerygma*), deed (*diakonia*), prayer and worship (*leiturgia*) and the everyday witness of the

Christian life (*martyria*); teaching as building up and strengthening people in their relationship with God and each other; and healing as wholeness and reconciliation into koinonia - communion with God, communion with people, and communion with creation as a whole".

Healing the wounds of church and mission history

52. When Christian churches speak of the healing ministry as an indispensable element of the body of Christ they must also face their own past and present, sharing a long and often conflictual history with each other. Church splits, rivalry in mission and evangelism, proselytism, exclusions of persons or whole churches for dogmatic reasons, condemnations of different church traditions anathematized as heretical movements, but also inappropriate collaboration between churches and political movements or economic and political powers, have left deep marks and wounds in many parts of the one body of Christ and continue to have a harmful impact on interdenominational relationships.

Christians and churches are still in deep need of healing and reconciliation with each other. The agenda of church unity remains an essential part of the healing ministry. The ecumenical movement has indeed been and still is one of the most promising and hope giving instruments for the necessary processes of healing and reconciliation within Christianity. What such processes mean and imply has been described in the document "Mission and the Ministry of Reconciliation" recommended by the CWME commission in 2004.[22]

The local Christian community as a primary place for the healing ministry

53. The Tübingen consultations in 1964 and 1967[23] affirmed that the local congregation or Christian community is the primary agent for healing. With all the need and legitimacy of specialized Christian institutions like hospitals, primary health services and special healing homes it was emphasized that every

Christian community as such - as the body of Christ - has a healing significance and relevance. The way people are received, welcomed and treated in a local community has a deep impact on its healing function. The way a network of mutual support, of listening and of mutual care is maintained and nurtured in a local congregation expresses the healing power of the church as a whole. All basic functions of the local church have a healing dimension also for the wider community: the proclamation of the word of God as a message of hope and comfort, the celebration of the eucharist as a sign of reconciliation and restoration, the pastoral ministry of each believer, individual or community intercessory prayer for all members and the sick in particular.[24] Each individual member in a local congregation has a unique gift to contribute to the overall healing ministry of the church.

The charismatic gifts of healing

54. According to the biblical tradition the Christian community is entrusted by the Holy Spirit with a great variety of spiritual gifts (1 Cor, 12) in which charisms relevant to the healing ministry have a prominent role. All gifts of healing within a given community need deliberate encouragement, spiritual nurture, education and enrichment but also a proper ministry of pastoral accompaniment and ecclesial oversight. Charisms are not restricted to the so-called "supernatural" gifts which are beyond common understanding and/or personal world-view, but hold to a wider understanding in which both talents and approaches of modern medicine, alternative medical approaches as well as gifts of traditional healing and spiritual forms of healing have their own right. Among the most important means and approaches to healing within Christian tradition mention should be made of

- the gift of praying for the sick and the bereaved;
- the gift of laying-on of hands;
- the gift of blessing;
- the gift of anointing with oil;
- the gift of confession and repentance;

- the gift of consolation;
- the gift of forgiveness;
- the gift of healing wounded memories;
- the gift of healing broken relationships and/or the family tree;
- the gift of meditative prayer;
- the gift of silent presence;
- the gift of listening to each other;
- the gift of opposing and casting out evil spirits (ministry of deliverance);
- the gift of prophecy (in the personal and socio-political realms).

The eucharist as the Christian healing event par excellence

55. The celebration of the eucharist is considered by the majority of Christians as the most prominent healing gift and unique healing act in the church in all her dimensions. While the essential contribution of the eucharist for healing is not understood in the same manner by all denominational traditions, the sacramental aspect of Christian healing is more deeply appreciated and expressed in many churches today. In the eucharist Christians experience what it means to be brought together and to be made one, constituted again as the body of Christ across social, linguistic and cultural barriers, however not yet across denominational divides. The remaining division between churches, which prevent a common celebration at the Lord's table is the reason why many Christians have difficulties in grasping and experiencing the eucharist as the healing event par excellence.

56. The eucharistic liturgy provides however the setting and visible expression for God's healing presence in the midst of the church and through her in mission to this broken world. The healing dimension of the eucharist is underscored by the tradition reaching back to the early church requesting reconciliation with the brother or sister prior to sharing the sacrament. It is expressed also through the mutual sharing of the peace and forgiveness of sins between God and the believers in the liturgy of confession. Very early evidence is also there for the Christian

practice to share the eucharist with the sick and to bring it to homes and hospitals. The body of Christ broken for the suffering world is received as the central gift of God's healing grace. Every eucharistic celebration restores both the community of the church and renews the healing gifts and charisms. According to ancient sources the liturgical tradition of anointing the sick with oil is rooted in the eucharistic celebration. In both Roman Catholic and Orthodox traditions the oil used for anointing the sick[25] is sanctified by the local bishop in the liturgy of benediction of the oil during holy week (chrismation mass), thereby rooting the healing ministry of the church both in the eucharist and in the cross and resurrection of Christ.

The healing dimension of worship in general and special healing services

57. For all Christian denominations and church traditions it holds true that the worshipping community and the worship itself can have a deep healing dimension. Opening oneself in praise and lament to God, joining the others as a community of believers, being liberated from guilt and burdens of life, experiencing even unbelievable cures, being enflamed by the experience of singing and of praise are a tremendously healing experience. It must however also be acknowledged that this can never be taken for granted. Inappropriate forms of Christian worship including triumphalistic "healing services" in which the healer is glorified at the expense of God and where false expectations are raised, can deeply hurt and harm people. In many places, still, special monthly or weekly services are experienced as authentic witness to God's healing power and care. Indeed, in such worship, explicit recognition is given to the needs of those seeking healing from experiences of loss, of fragmentation, of despair or physical illness. In many church traditions worship events combine the eucharist with the ritual of personal prayer for the sick and the laying-on of hands and are an appropriate response both to the mandate of the church and the longing for healing within the population. The contribution of

Pentecostalism and the charismatic movement both within and outside the historical churches to the contemporary renewal of the understanding of the healing dimension of worship and of mission in general has to be acknowledged in this context.

Deepening a common understanding of a Christian healing spirituality

58. It is clear for all Christian traditions that Christian healing ministries cannot be seen as mere techniques and professional skills or certain rituals. All of them depend on a Christian spirituality and discipline which influences all spheres of personal as well as professional life. Such spirituality depends on faith in God, following Christ's footsteps, on how the body is treated, how the limitations of space and time are dealt with, how pain and sickness are coped with, how one eats and fasts, prays and meditates visits the sick, helps the needy and keeps silence in openness to God's Spirit.

There is a need for discernment as to what constitutes authentic Christian spirituality. There exist theologies and forms of Christian practice that do not contribute to healing. Distorted forms of spirituality or piety can lead to unhealthy lives and questionable relationship with God and fellow human beings.

The ordained and the laity in the healing ministry

59. In many congregations it can be observed that only ordained people are allowed to extend signs of blessing and prayers of healing for people who are in need. Biblical evidence reminds us however that the Spirit and the Spirit's gifts have been promised to all members of the people of God (Acts 2:17, 1 Cor. 12:3ff.) and that every member of the church is called to participate in the healing ministry. Churches are encouraged to support the gifts and potentials particularly of lay people both in local congregations as well as in health-care institutions. Empowering people to act as ambassadors of the healing ministry is an essential task of both the ordained ministers and dea-

cons in the church as well as the Christian professionals working in various health related institutions.

60. How each church can best recognize the mandate of the local community, express the responsibility of the ordained ministry and of lay people in the healing ministry, depends on its own tradition and structure. The Church of England has e.g. appointed in many places a healing adviser on the level of the diocese. This minister is responsible for encouragement, education and also spiritual and pastoral advice for emerging healing ministries in cooperation with the regional bishop. The healing ministry of the church thereby receives a visible recognition and support in the church as a whole instead of just being delegated to specialized institutions or restricted to the local situation.

The need for educating Christians for the healing ministry - integration versus compartmentalization

61. There is a growing consensus that education for the different forms of Christian healing ministry is not as widespread and developed as it ought to be in the various sectors of church life. Explicit teaching on a Christian understanding of healing in many programmes of theological education is absent or still underdeveloped. However recently efforts have been made to include HIV/AIDS in the curricula of institutions of theological education in Africa. But many training and educational programmes are taking place only within the different fields of specialized competence. Nurses, doctors, diaconical workers are educated within their own professional fields. There is no interaction between different education programmes and fields of competencies, and there is a lack to introduce issues and basic themes of Christian healing within the mainline stream of ministerial and adult education in general.

The healing ministry of the community and healing professions

62. The deliberations of the consultations at Tübingen in 1964 and 1967 and the setting up of the Christian Medical Commission in

1968, with the development of the concept of Primary Health Care (PHC) in the 1980s created a PHC movement that began with great hope for change, but has not been sustained. The divide created between high technology based medicine on the one hand and primary health care on the other has been detrimental to the struggle for a better and healthier world. While committed Christian professionals developed outstanding programmes in primary health care, the congregational involvement in the PHC movement was patchy and minimal. Though the access and justice issues were addressed to some extent in that movement, the spiritual aspects were not addressed appropriately. Traditional systems of medicine in many countries have been unnecessarily condemned by the modern allopathic system of medicine and have developed in isolation and in competition to it, creating problems of relation between Christian communities and traditional health specialists.

63. Additional dramatic changes in society and health systems have brought increased tensions in recent years for many of those who are working within the established medical systems, in particular in industrialized countries and centres. Increasing pressures to rationalize health care, to reduce costs and medical personnel tend to prevent doctors, nurses and assistants to relate to a holistic approach in health and healing. At the same time, the need for addressing the whole person in health care has become more than obvious in many parts of the world. How medical personnel will be able to respond to these contradictory requests remains an open question. It is encouraging to discern signs and signals of a new quest and openness for cooperation with religious organizations, particularly Christian churches, in many secular institutions of the established health system.

64. Christian churches should be open and receptive to listen and learn from the situation of those facing the ever more growing contradictions and shortcomings within the established medical systems.

The health professionals on their part should recognize that health issues move beyond the individual to the community which is a social network with many resources and skills that can promote health. Health professionals are challenged to see themselves as part of a broader network of healing disciplines that include the medical, technical, social and psychological sciences, as well as religions and traditional approaches to healing. This wider view will help the professionals to integrate suffering into the concept of health and enable people with incurable physical problems to be healed persons. It will also encourage the health professionals to share information with and empower the patient to feel responsible and take decisions for their own health.

65. The primary health care approach in the community should be backed by adequate secondary and tertiary care facilities. The referral system should be reciprocal and mutually supportive.

Healing ministry and advocacy

66. While this document concentrates on the medical and spiritual aspects of the healing ministry, it acknowledges that there exists a wider definition of healing which includes efforts of persons, movements, societies and churches for fundamental transformation of structures which produce poverty, exploitation, harm and sickness or illness. The earlier CMC study of 1990[26] is still considered a valid guideline for that wider aspect of the healing ministry, which gained even more urgency with the HIV/AIDS pandemic. The 1990 document considers health to be a justice issue, an issue of peace, and an issue related to the integrity of creation. Consequently it requests a healing congregation to "take the healing ministry into the political, social and economic arenas:

- advocating the elimination of oppression, racism and injustice;

- supporting peoples' struggle for liberation;

- joining others of goodwill in growing together in social awareness;

- creating public opinion in support of the struggle for justice in health". [27]

67. All Christians, especially those active in healing ministries and in medical professions, those gifted with the charisms of prophecy, are called to be advocates for such a holistic approach on national and international political scenes. Because of their specific competence and experience, they bear a special responsibility to speak with and on behalf of the marginalized and the underprivileged and contribute to strengthen advocacy networks and campaigns to put pressure on international organizations, governments, industries and research institutions, so that the present scandalous handling of resources be fundamentally challenged and modified.

Training

68. Because of all these aspects of the church's mission in terms of health and care, training for medical and health professionals will be a key area for appropriate action. Congregations and those who work in the pastoral areas too need training on the holistic approaches to health and the specific contributions they can make as alluded to in this document.

69. The challenge is for Christians to continue to engage communities in such a way as to incorporate the pedagogy of healing in the church, so as to:

- motivate and mobilize communities to identify the core issues of ill health, to own the issues and to take effective action;

- identify with the holistic understanding of the healing ministry in the gospel;

- work with wider societies to bring about difference in peoples health and life.

5. Open Questions and Necessary Debates

70. This chapter contains items on which there is ongoing debate among Christians from different denominational traditions

and/or cultural backgrounds. This does not mean that all affirmations below are contested. But the scope and consequences of some are subject of debate.

All healing comes from God: Christian healing spirituality and non-Christian healing practices

71. That all healing comes from God is a conviction shared by most if not all Christian traditions.[28] There is however a debate as to the consequence of such an affirmation for the approach of people and traditions or healing practices of other religions.

72. Affirming the presence of God's healing energies at work in the whole of creation, thanks and praise should be given for all different means, approaches and traditions which contribute to the healing of human persons, communities as well as creation, by reinforcing their healing potentials.

73. In many contexts where a strong longing for healing is felt both within as well as outside the Christian churches, the question of Christian openness towards and reliance on healing practices rooted in other religions (such as various traditional religious medicinal approaches, but also Yoga, Reiki, Shiatsu, Zen-Meditation etc.) is however much debated within churches and Christian health related institutions. To what extent is Christian healing spirituality compatible with healing practices from other religions? Are those reconcilable and in harmony with basic principles of Christian spirituality?

74. Christian spirituality should show openness to all means of healing offered as part of God's ongoing creation. At the same time there are healing practices which associate themselves with a religious world-view which can be in contrast to basic Christian principles, and some Christians are particularly attentive to such dangers. For other Christians still, caution is requested, because evil spiritual powers might disguise their destroying effect behind apparently beneficial healing practices.

75. No healing practice is just neutral. It needs critical theological assessment. This is not to say that any Yoga or Reiki practices e.g. have no place in Christian parish centres. They can be practised, many Christians in the West believe, in ways which do not lead to a dissolution or fundamental distortion of Christian faith and the Christian community. The church has always been aware that God can reveal aspects of how creation works and contributes to healing through peoples of other languages, cultures and even religious traditions and this also applies to the realm of medical treatment, alternative medicine and alternative healing practices.

76. But caution or even explicit rejection are recommended wherever

- religious dependency is created on the healer or Guru;

- absolute spiritual, social or economic obedience is demanded;

- human beings are kept in a spirit of threat, anxiety or bondage due to healing practices;

- the success of a healing is made dependant on fundamental changes in the religious world-view of Christians.

77. As the biblical tradition shows, Christians are invited and commissioned to test everything, hold on to the good and abstain from every kind of evil (1 Thess. 5:21-22). When encountering practices of healing and energetic therapeutic work rooted in other religions, Christians should always first of all feel encouraged to rediscover the rich diversity and ancient spiritual traditions of healing within the Christian church itself.

Debate on the concepts of demonology and power encounter

78. Traditionally, the term "demonology" in Christian theology has been part of the doctrine of angels (angelology). Demons/demonic powers denote the "dark" side of spiritual reality.

The term "power[s]" in theological and ecumenical discourse is used in more than one way. Often and in particular in ecumenical circles it is used in relation to political violence and oppressive social structures

79. Among Pentecostal-charismatic Christians - but also beyond, among those who continue in the tradition of classical Christianity - the term "powers" usually mean spiritual powers, evil spirits, demons. Consequently "power encounter" is understood as an encounter between the (spiritual) power of God and other gods/spiritual realities. These Christians believe that the true God will show off God's power over others. While it is important that such dialogue does not simplify the complex intricacies of spirit worlds thriving in - and alongside - the age of post-modernism it should at the same time resist any attempt to turn the Holy Spirit into a powerful means to an end as if the church had to vindicate God.[29] The church is to witness for the living God. She has not to prove God right.

80. An ecumenical challenge to the churches is to acknowledge the various meanings assigned to the talk about powers and try to resist reductionism. While the traditional way of relating "powers" to spiritual forces seems to be the primary biblical connotation, the understanding of powers in terms of social and political realities is also present in the Bible (cf. e.g. the temptation story in Matt. 4:1-11 and Luke 4:1-13) and can be seen as a legitimate interpretation of the Christian message.

81. The Pentecostal-charismatic interest in power encounter poses serious challenges and can be subject to theological and pastoral concerns. The idea of "power encounter" as explained above may lead to a triumphalistic, aggressive presentation of the gospel. In some cases, "spirits" are attributed influence and power beyond what appear to be appropriate theologically, blurring the meaning of individual and collective responsibility.

82. This being the case, demonology and exorcisms present cognitive and spiritual challenges to those churches whose frame of

reference and theology is shaped by a post-Enlightenment scientific rationality as is that world-view to the one explaining events through referring to spiritual beings. An appropriate intercultural and ecumenical dialogue for the sake of the churches' ministry of healing as a whole seems urgent.

Sharing resources and insights in Christian healing within the ecumenical fellowship

83. Many church traditions have their own rich insights and liturgical as well as theological treasures and can contribute to a holistic understanding and new appreciation of the Christian ministry of health and healing today. The Anglican, Orthodox and Roman Catholic traditions offer distinct and different healing liturgies. It is encouraged to make these known among other denominations and traditions and to share such formulas which exist within the ecumenical community of churches.

Study and dialogue on demonology

84. It would be a worthwhile task for the WCC mission desk toinitiate a wide-scale study process on the topic of demonology and powers since, as mentioned, it is a topic that Christians and Christian communities are tackling in their everyday life. One part of the study task would be to consider the issue of rehabilitating the office of exorcist as Christian ministry in those church traditions where it does not exist.

Ecumenical initiative on healing spirituality

85. It could be well considered whether for the years to come an ecumenical initiative is needed to deepen the Christian healing spirituality and to encourage related formation courses for voluntary workers, professional health-care workers and ordained ministers.

The need for round tables on the future of health, spirituality and healing

86. Established institutions of health care in many countries are in a process of transformation and institutional crisis, partly due to economic factors and financial instability, lack of proper management and leadership, rising costs of high technology medicine, changed patterns in the behaviour of patients, lack of compliance of the patients and the demographic imbalances in many Western societies. Historically speaking Christian mission had played a pioneering role in bringing about and shaping the health systems in many countries of the South. It also has a responsibility in contributing to overcoming the crisis of the established institutions of health care at the beginning of the 21st century. In accordance with the tradition of the Christian Medical Commission and recent proposals[30] it is recommended that the various Christian medical commissions and associations existent in the different regions of the world join hands and establish interdisciplinary dialogue forums on the future of health care and health systems both in the West as well as in the South. Ways of exchanging and strengthening the collaboration between the various regional Christian medical associations should be sought in order to give new profile to the Christian ministry of healing and make it more visible and effective before the eyes of the world.

1 CWME conference preparatory paper no. 10, on: www.mission2005.org

2 Cf. Christina de Vries: "The Global Health Situation: Priorities for the Churches' Health Ministry beyond AD 2000", *International Review of Mission,* vol. 90, nos 356-357, pp.149ff.

3 For the WCC definition, see §31 below.

4 World Health Organization (WHO): *The World Health Report - Changing History* , Geneva, 2004.

5 United Nations: Report on Millennium Development Goals. Cf. www.un.org/millenniumgoals/ Reference is made here to #4: reduce by two-thirds the mortality rate among children under five; #5: reduce by three-quarters the maternal mortality ratio; # 6: Halt and begin to reverse the spread of HIV/AIDS. Halt and begin to reverse the incidence of malaria and other major diseases.

6 WHO, *op.cit.*

7 Cf. *Healing and Wholeness. The Churches' Role in Health. The report of a study by the Christian Medical Commission,* WCC, 1990. Document received by the WCC central committee. Quote from page 1.

8 Such as fast-food and other consumption trends leading to overweight of children and adults in affluent societies, addiction to drugs, overconsumption of TV and video, etc.

9 Cf. Harold G. Koeching, Michael E. Muccullogh, David B. Lason eds, Handbook of Religion and Health, New York, Oxford UP, 2001.

10 The question of the relation between gospel and cultures was seriously addressed at the world mission conference in Salvador in 1996, cf. Christopher Duraisingh ed., *Called to One Hope: The Gospel in Diverse Cultures,* WCC, 1998.

11 A conception developed in particular by Paul Tillich. Cf. Paul Tillich: "The meaning of health" (1961) in *idem, Writings in the Philosophy of Culture/ Kulturphilosophische Schriften (Main works/Hauptwerke 2)* ed. by M. Palmer, Berlin-New York, 1990, pp.342-52. *Paul Tillich,* "The relation of religion and health. Historical considerations and theoretical questions" (1946), in *ibid.,* pp.209-38. *Idem, Systematic Theology III. Life and the Spirit, History and the Kingdom of God,* Chicago, 1963, pp.275-82.

12 CMC study on "Healing and Wholeness", p.6.

13 One example are the discussions around the conception of "salutogenesis" developed by the medical sociologist Aaron Antonowsky, focusing on what helps maintaining health and well-being in body and soul, instead of focussing on factors producing illness.

14 *A Time to Heal: A Report for the House of Bishops of the General Synod of the Church of England on the Healing Ministry,* London, Church House Publ., 2000.

15 *Mission in Context. Transformation -Reconciliation - Empowerment. An LWF Contribution to the Understanding and Practice of Mission,* Geneva, LWF, 2004, pp.39-40.

16 Cf. IRM, vol. 93, nos 370-371, July-Oct. 2004 on "Divine Healing, Pentecostalism and Mission".

17 Take as an example the CMC study of 1990, Healing and Wholeness, op. cit.

18 Group report from a consultation with Pentecostals in Ghana in 2002, published in IRM, July-Oct. 2004, p.371.

19 See below, ch. 5.

20 This refers to congregations, as well as church-related health care institutions and specialized diaconical services.

21 CWME conference preparatory document no. 1.

22 CWME conference preparatory document no. 10.

23 Two consultations held at the German Institute for Medical Mission (Difäm) in Tübingen, Germany, who were at the origin of the creation of the Christian Medical Commission and the health work of the WCC. Cf. *The Healing Church. The Tübingen consultation 1964,* WCC, 1965, and James C. McGilvray, *The Quest for Health and Wholeness,* Tübingen, Difäm, 1981.

24 Cf. the excellent chapter on healing community in the CMC document "Healing and Wholeness", pp.31f.

25 It was only in the middle ages that they were narrowed down to a sacramental sign reserved to the dying as "extreme unction".

26 *Healing and Wholeness.*

27 *Ibid.,* p.32.

28 Cf. IRM July-Oct. 2004 (dialogue with Pentecostals); cf. also LWF mission statement , p.39. The affirmation that all healing comes from God is already to be found in the documents resulting from the Tübingen consultation of 1964, cf. *The Healing Church,* p.36.

29 God vindicates the church instead. Matt. 10:19-20; Luke 21:15; Mark. 13:11.

30 Cf. results of the consultation held in Hamburg in 2000, published in *IRM* , vol. 90, nos 356-357, Jan.-April 2001, on the theme "Health, Faith and Healing".